SILICON SIMULACRA

POST-HUMANS OF THE MACHINE WORLDS

LEN ELLIS

ISBN: 1449980864
ISBN-13: 9781449980863

LCCN: 2010904257

For my parents

ACKNOWLEDGEMENTS

The following publishers granted permission to reprint excerpts from their books in this one.

Excerpt from *Collected Poems,* copyright © 1940 and copyright renewed © 1968, by W. H. Auden, reprinted by permission of Random House, Inc.

Excerpt from *One Human Minute,* copyright © 1986, by Stanislaw Lem, English translation copyright © 1986 by Catherine Leach, reprinted by permission of Houghton Miflin Harcourt Publishing Company

Except from *Bureau of Inverse Technology, Suicide Box, Engineer's Report,* by Natalie Jeremijenko, reprinted by permission of Natalie Jeremijenko.

Excerpt from *Painting by the Numbers: Komar and Melamid's Scientific Guide to Art,* copyright © 1997, by Joanne Wypijewski, reprinted by permission of Farrar Straus, and Giroux.

CONTENTS

PREFACE

Like many liberal arts PhDs who couldn't find a decent paying job in academia, I drifted into marketing and earned a good living working at big Madison Avenue agencies. Most of my career was spent on the leading edge, doing data-based and online marketing, and one thing kept gnawing at me: the consumer-like entities with whom I was communicating—data profiles and cyberpersonas—were as a matter of fact part human and part machine. I looked for a book about these hybrid entities but couldn't find one. So, I wrote one. At the end of the day, the result seemed worth sharing.

Although the text combines my academic and business backgrounds, it doesn't advance scholarship and won't improve anyone's ROI. Rather, it seeks to complement the literatures of both communities. For academics, the examination of real-world practices puts meat on the bones of their largely theoretical arguments, of course with the messiness for which the real world is well known. Conversely, these theoretical arguments reveal to marketers dimensions and trajectories of their real-world practices that are outside their conceptual frameworks, naturally with the abstraction for which ivory-tower thinking is well known.

The perception of hybrid entities, emerging within databases and networks, could only be presented as an essay, one person's working out of a topic. So the aim is to make a plausible argument and do so in language as plain as the topic allows. Accordingly, the text examines closely the assumptions, mechanics and dynamics of our virtual versions but largely ignores their rapidly evolving technical details. The omissions of greater substance are multiplayer games and virtual worlds. Role-playing in immersive environments through customized avatars is a novel arena for social interaction that one day may have broad implications, but it's currently a niche interest. Meanwhile, our silicon simulacra apply to everyone, are here today and are no game.

In developing this analysis, I borrowed a lot from others. The notes acknowledge them. For readers who want to delve deeper, the notes often include references to others' works on the same topics as well as occasional bibliographic comments. For the record, these references do not imply that the authors cited would agree with the arguments advanced here. The bibliography is limited to works that were quoted in the text or especially important to its arguments. All Web pages referenced in the notes and bibliography were accessible as of February 2010. To facilitate sharing portions of the book's argument, individual chapters are available as PDF files at www.siliconsimulacra.com

Various friends, relatives, co-workers and teachers read parts of the manuscript along the way, and their comments helped me strengthen and clarify its arguments. These generous folks include Andrew Ellis, Tess Harris, Max Kalehoff, Richard Kluger, Rebecca Lieb, Michael Lydon, Lois Lynn, Allan Silver and Brooke Knight Warner. Erin Brenner did an excellent job in preparing the manuscript for publication, as did the team at CreateSpace, Amazon's print-on-demand company. Any deficiencies rest, of course, with the author.

March 2010
New York City

INTRODUCTION

If a man would rather be a machine, I cannot
argue with him. He is a different being from me.
> —Samuel Johnson in James Boswell, *The Life*
> *of Samuel Johnson* (1858)

What is used as an element in a machine
is in fact an element in a machine.
> —Norbert Weiner, *The Human Use of Human*
> *Beings* (1950)

As far back in time as we know, humans and our tools
have been interrelated. Our hominid precursors invented
tools approximately 2 million years ago and altered the
course of their evolution. Over the next 1.8 million years,
their success with tools changed the pressures of natural se-
lection and played a causal role in the emergence of *Homo
sapiens* and our physiology—our bipedalism, brain size, pel-
vic structure and other physical features.[1] Ever since, we've
been inventing tools, machines and technologies that augment our powers. But until recently, humans and our devices have been separate.

Today, scientists are busy blurring that boundary. Some
are trying to upload the human brain, encoding its opera-
tions into computers to enable these machines to think,
even learn; that branch of computer science is called artificial intelligence. Others are working in the field of virtual
reality, physically sticking their heads and hands into machines via head-mounted displays and data gloves that feed
images, sounds and other signals directly into the human
sensorium.

While these pursuits are on the leading edge, the rest
of us, at least in the wired nations, are already immersed

from the neck up in two of the biggest technologies ever invented: the datascape and cyberspace. The former refers to the vast array of business and government computers where data about every one of us is processed, stored, exchanged, combined, analyzed and then acted upon. The latter refers to the worldwide network of interlinked computers, through which everyone can connect with everyone else.

Both the datascape and cyberspace are close to the concept of technology as explored by Martin Heidegger in "The Question Concerning Technology." As a philosopher, Heidegger tried to grasp the essence of technology, the particular claim of *all* technology *everywhere* and *always*, regardless of any specific purposes and properties. That essence is mastery, and it poses two inherent dangers: it's expansionist and reductionist. That is, technology will take from the world anything it needs and reduce it into a means to an end. It's a way of being in the world that sets up and brings forth all things so they are available as a stockpile of manipulatable resources on call for instrumental use. The datascape and cyberspace are specific instances; they set up and bring forth humans in particular ways to, with and for others' use. But there's a crucial difference. For Heidegger, human and machine were still subject and object. In the datascape and in cyberspace the human subject is reconstituted inside the machine as an element of the object.[2]

In popular science fiction the nightmare of humankind being subjugated by a marching army of androids has been superseded by the threat of being assimilated into human-machine collectives, like "the Borg" from the television series *Star Trek: The Next Generation* or "The Matrix" of the Hollywood movie series—hive-like amalgams of flesh and metal, blood and data, that are both self and society at once. That future of human assimilation into the machine is reality today. All of us are already reconstituted inside the datascape as data profiles and in cyberspace as cyberpersonas.

These simulacra are hybrid entities. They are part human. We continually update both the datascape and cyberspace, and as we change, our simulacra change in tandem. And they are part machine. In the datascape we appear as probabilities of behavior, an informational output; in cyberspace, we appear as patterns of connections, a network effect. The data profile and cyberpersona are our machine appearances, the forms in which these two machines set us up and bring us forth to, with and for others within them. How we stand relative to each differs. We are largely passive in the datascape. The powerful call us up as probabilities to inform their decision making. We are largely active in cyberspace. We create our own patterns as we present ourselves to and connect with others. Before examining when and how our simulacra came to be, how they re-present us and what opportunities and challenges each poses, the self they re-present needs its own introduction.

The Modern Self

The self we know and to whom many still aspire—the continuous, whole and bounded individual whose will is exercised in choice and action—did not always exist. He (sic) emerged with the modernization of Western society, a transformation that began in the 16th century and reached maturity in the early 20th. At the end of the 20th century, this self started to disappear and may be gone altogether in the 21st. Here's the gist of that history.

The foundational ethos of modern Western culture was humanism, the belief that Man possesses an end of his own and that human agency is the source of hope, critique and progress, the engine of history and the locus of emancipation. That ethos was a recipe for continual change and what happened over four centuries of modernization was this: The Reformation, Renaissance, Scientific Revolution, French Revolution and Industrial Revolution gave rise to the nation state, the spread of market capitalism and the emergence of mass urban society.

Two features distinguished how modernity organized human affairs. One was the chunking up of social life into separate realms—church and state, government and commerce, work and leisure, knowledge and labor, science and art—with institutions and practices specific to each. The most basic division, ubiquitous and a given for the others, was that between the public and private spheres and the types of relationships that prevailed in each. The public sphere, largely government and commerce, was organized using *impersonal* relationships, such as transactions, contracts, laws, rules and other standardized procedures, that were to govern the pursuit of power and wealth among *replaceable* persons. The private sphere, largely family, lovers and friends, consisted of *personal* relationships—unguarded expressions of intimacy, affection and generosity—based on the unique qualities of *irreplaceable* persons.[3]

Modernity's second distinguishing feature was to cast the individual as the irreducible unit of both spheres but in two modes, pursuing self-interest in the public sphere and self-expression in the private. In modernity's public sphere, individualism meant the equality of all, a radical idea at the time. In the medieval period, collective life and one's station in that life were organized by hierarchal social bonds defined by birthright and custom, such as the privileges of the estates, the control of commerce by guilds, the coercion of faith by the clergy and others. Champions of modernity characterized these social relationships as artificial and restrictive, arguing instead that all men were fundamentally alike, sharing an essential and constant nature, and should enjoy the status and rights appropriate to all men. Once the 18th century secured the equality of all men in the public realm, the 19th century turned to the uniqueness of each individual in the private sphere. What was general to all became the ability of each to be this and no other individual. The incomparable self, realized largely in the private sphere, was how the universal found expression in the 19th century.

Working out the two individualisms was a central theme of modern Western culture. Self-interest with its calculating instrumental rationality is usually traced back to René

Descartes' "detached thinker" and then forward to the enlightened self-interest upon which John Locke based a liberal political philosophy and Adam Smith based his theory of self-regulating markets. Self expression with its inner outpourings is usually traced back to Jean-Jacques Rousseau's "natural man" and then forward into Romanticism, most notably among English and German poets, yielding our modern concepts of art, genius and individuality. In summary, modernity entailed two modes of individualism: the equality of all in pursuing self-interest through impersonal relationships with replaceable others in the public sphere and the uniqueness of each in pursuing self-expression through personal relationships with irreplaceable others in the private sphere.[4]

No sooner had the individual became established as the irreducible unit of both spheres than the assumptions about the world on which he was based came under diverse and ultimately fatal attacks. Karl Marx the social thinker, not the political agitator, launched the first attack in the mid-19th century. He killed off Culture with a compelling argument that our material conditions, especially for Marx the regime of production, shape the ideals to which we aspire as well as how we express our aspirations. Around the same time Charles Darwin knocked off both Man and Nature. He demoted Man to man, surrendering our unique status in the universe in exchange for a small branch in the animal kingdom, and he recast Nature as an engine blindly selecting for survival those individual variations better suited to local conditions. Two decades later God died. Friedrich Nietzsche wrote His obituary in 1882 and included all the other external moralities of good and evil. Early in the new century, Science lost its truth status when Albert Einstein bumped off Isaac Newton by proving that space and time were not absolute concepts but were instead relative to the observer. Meanwhile Freud led us to doubt the Self. We could no longer believe the reasons that we professed to account for our actions; they were likely rationalizations, sublimations or some other distortion of inner urges. The coup de grace was World War I's massive butchery. Machine guns, mustard gas, tanks and aeroplanes blew up what was left of our 19th century ideals: the chivalric holdovers of honor and glory, the belief that technology per se meant improvement and the legitimacy of lesser authorities, civil, religious and familial.

The systematic unraveling of our truths took up most of the 20th century. The liberal arts, including history and literature, and the social sciences, including anthropology, economics and sociology, were deconstructed, revealing foundations built not on universal truths but on local ideals, resulting in baked-in "biases." Within just a few generations, the entire Western canon was trashed as the ideology of dead white males, masking, by accident or by design, racism, sexism, colonialism and imperialism, while humanism itself was derided as misguided hubris. As for the physical sciences, after Einstein, they all went "relative to the observer." Truths were no longer givens in Nature waiting to be revealed but were instead replicable answers to specific questions posed by particular people in particular times and places for particular purposes. In short, nothing was ever discovered. Everything was always invented. Such bedrock concepts as empiricism, objectivity, experimentation and measurement still produced practical and reliable answers to the questions posed, but now the answers and the questions that conjured them into existence are understood as socially constructed.

The *death of God* is the smart set's shorthand for modernity outsmarting itself into relativism — everything is as meaningful as everything else—and into nihilism—human life and history have no grand purpose, meaning or destiny. In casting off God, Man, Nature, Science and all the other universal, eternal and certain higher truths and grand narratives, modernity also cast the individual adrift. A frequently quoted passage from Albert Camus' *The Myth of Sisyphus* describes our malaise midway through the 20th century: "In a universe divested of illusions and light, man feels an alien, a stranger. His exile is without remedy since he is deprived of the memory of a lost home or the hope of a promised land."

Today, rudderless relativism is the new normal. The ongoing proliferation of media, publicizing myriad perspectives, proves repeatedly every day that no one truth exists. Similarly, late-modern aesthetics embraces a world of many truths and, so, favors collage and pastiche in art and fusion and mixture in music. Ethics bend the same way, toward detachment, irony and the easy acceptance of a plurality of pleasures, none of which has meaning superior to the others. Hardly anyone today asks meaning-of-life questions—where we come from, why we're here and where we're going—because hardly anyone believes that truths are available to answer those questions. Instead, a late-night TV comedian jokes about truthinesss: "something that seems like truth—the truth we want to exist." This resonates so broadly, it was named Word of the Year by the American Dialect Society in 2005 and by Merriam-Webster in 2006.

Not only are the grand narratives in disarray, but our little lives as producers and consumers are in a tizzy as well. No longer do we expect to stay at one company for a lifetime and retire with a gold watch and a company pension. All jobs today are temporary, and we're told that our skills must be portable and that we must be open to and adept at re-skilling so we can plug into new opportunities as they arise. Similarly, the one-size-fits-all American Dream that the World War II generation shared was succeeded by the marketing of difference, at first to groups, then to segments and niches, tomorrow to markets of one. Modernity premised the individual as the irreducible unit of everything and, thanks largely to modernity, it's the only thing we can lay claim to.

And even that claim is slipping away. The individual as the hero of modernism—owner of his own person and capabilities, whose autonomous will is exercised in choice and action in the polity, economy and family—was always theoretical rather than actual. From the very birth of modernity, everyone knew that "no man is an island, entire to itself," while much of modern social science has focused on proving just how much of our individuality is neither singular nor original but is instead molded by and with others through such patterns of social interaction as acculturation, socialization, reference groups, peer pressure, significant others, other-directedness and status seeking. Nurture as much as nature shapes each of us, we now believe, inside and out-.

In today's late-modern age we even question the existence of an individual subjectivity that is bounded off from others. According to appraisals associated with theories of phenomenology in philosophy, deconstruction in literary criticism and post-structuralism in linguistics, the "in here" of each of us exists in language. Like the fish doesn't know it's in water, we can't easily apprehend that each of us comes to consciousness within language and that every thought and feeling is a borrowing from, a reconfiguration of and a re-presentation of what's already there, prefigured, in language. Just as the "out theres" of history, physics, sociology, biology and so on are now seen as socially constructed by and within communities of interpretation, so too each individual's "in here" is no longer seen as bounded off from others but as co-created with others from within language.

While this perspective reframes the self's subjectivity as inter-subjective, it still leaves one boundary intact, the boundary between the world of subjects and the world of objects, between humans and things. The two phenomena examined here cross this boundary in and across our everyday life. Each of us is already immersed in the datascape and increasingly immersed in cyberspace, and each of us is reconstituted by and within each machine as data profiles and cyberpersonas, respectively.[5]

These hybrid entities are this book's foreground, the describable and comprehensible manifestations of the larger phenomenon that can be glimpsed in the background, the assimilation of humans to machines and the emergence of the post-human. This new term refers to an entity that comes from and is continually nourished by the carbon-based world but is disembodied, shaped by and for the silicon-based world. The vector from carbon to silicon is information, and the resulting entity lacks the boundaries, coherence and destiny of singular individuals. It is instead composed of heterogeneous components that are subject to continuous construction and reconstruction and that manifest different identities under different perspectives.[6] This post-human form is the way we are set up and brought forth in both machine worlds, but the particulars of each are the place to begin.

Data Profiles

Profiles of us made in the datascape make many people uneasy. One issue is power, our sense that calculations, judgments and decisions about us are being made behind the scenes in unknown ways that could be damaging and over which we have no control. Initially, government was the threat. In Franz Kafka's novel *The Trial* (1916—1917, published posthumously in 1925), a judicial court has accused and arrested the protagonist but will not reveal what information it has, what decisions it's making or what crimes it's charging; the ordeal is a nightmare. A no less chilling everyday reality was described in *Cancer Ward* (1968) by Alexander Solzenitsyn:

> As every man goes through life he fills in a number of forms for the record, each containing a number of questions ... There are thus hundreds of little threads radiating from every man, millions of threads in all. If these threads were suddenly to become visible, the whole sky would look like a spider's Web, and if they materialized as rubber bands, buses, trams and even people would all lose the ability to move, and the wind would be unable to carry torn-up newspapers or autumn leaves along the streets of the city. They are not visible, they are not material, but every man is constantly aware of

their existence ... Each man, permanently aware of his own invisible threads, naturally develops a respect for the people who manipulate threads.[7]

In the 1970s Western European nations and the United State—the former, systematically, the latter, haphazardly—started putting limits on the state's use of data. Today, even when aimed at protecting citizens from terrorists, government initiatives with data analytics are criticized as profiling, while its use of personally identifiable information is curbed on privacy grounds. We have many watchdogs to protect our liberties against government encroachment, as we should, but data in that same decade escaped the boundaries of governments and their bureaucracies. That's when businesses, large and small, enabled by the availability of low-cost computing and consumer-level data, began parsing us into data-based profiles.

Consumers know the parts of this commercial practice that we can see. We know that most of the data are the electronic detritus that we leave behind in the process of consuming whenever we pay with plastic, browse a Web site, use a frequent shopper card, request information, submit claims, use a cell phone, return a warranty card, enter a sweepstakes, fill out a survey and act in any other way that surrenders data to merchants. We also know the general purpose of their data-crunching—to enable businesses to determine which goods and services, which incentives and benefits, they should offer to whom—because we're on the receiving end. Some also know that this data travels; it's bought, sold and combined with still other data to create profiles of us that suit the still different purposes of still other marketers.

Privacy defenders decry this practice but their accusations are ill grounded and misleading. Data-based profiles are not individual dossiers. Profiles describe groups, aggregates of hypothetical "persons" statistically defined as more likely than others to behave in some way desired by a marketer. These groups are created to enable marketers to differentiate these persons from those persons and to treat them differently, justified by optimizing profits or efficiency. Of course, statistical differentiation in the service of commercial discrimination engenders problems of fairness and transparency. These are not privacy issues, however. Rather, they speak to how the method is used and as such are rather superficial. The deeper issues with data-based marketing are rooted in the assumptions of social statistics, the older and more general method for using numbers to apprehend human affairs of which marketing analytics is a commercial version.

The first chapter recounts how this lens was developed in the 19th century to help particular people achieve particular purposes. It reveals the two limitations that are intrinsic to this method and that persist today. First, social statistics measures and predicts frequencies of individual variability within populations. It cannot explain, much less predict, anything at all about individuals. Second, the data that are rolled up into statistics are created by performing radical surgery on reality. Creating any datum requires such surgery but, when applied to human affairs, the process cannot capture much of what actually matters most to humans—our ideals, aspirations, possibilities and other qualitative future-facing drivers of human nature and action. The disappearance of individuals' qualities and possibilities was loudly criticized at the birth of the social statistics, as was the peril in this practice: the more prevalent data-based decision making about human affairs becomes, the more it tends to erode the legitimacy of those other ways of apprehending human affairs that do address those matters and push them into the shadows.

Roughly a century later, the data-based view of human affairs did become nearly ubiquitous in the wildly successful commercial practice of data-based marketing. The second chapter is a brief history of this development. Starting in the 1970s, the advent of the Information Age, especially the availability of low-cost data about individual consumers and their households and low-cost data processing, made this type of marketing possible. It was an economic crisis, however, that made it advantageous. Specifically, this way of framing and addressing consumers helped rescue the entire U.S. economy by turning it away from mass-manufacturing and mass-marketing the American Dream to the manufacturing of variety and the marketing of difference. Its success in parsing us by our differences in order to predict who among us are most likely to buy what products is the unsung hero of this tectonic shift. Over the last four decades, it helped drive consumer spending to over 70 percent of U.S. gross domestic product while driving its own growth to roughly half of all external spending by U.S. marketers.

The third chapter of the book's first half examines the three ways in which marketers address us: how all marketing communications conjures us up as self-expressionists; then, more narrowly, how advertising conjures us up as daydreamers; finally and quite closely, how data-based marketing conjures us up as probabilities.

Probabilistic profiles of ersatz "persons" provide the basis for almost all marketing decision making today, and all of us are conjured up, thousands of times daily, as some constellation of attributes that define some of us as more likely than others to fulfill some marketer's desire. Consider, for example, a college grad with liquid assets of $200,000 living in a mid-sized city, a mother with a cat and a European car and a head of household operating a home office. These are not three people, they're three profiles of the same person, created by three different marketers, each for his own purpose. Marketers work the datascape like a kaleidoscope, continually churning us into profiles, and we're never the same person twice. Indeed, we're never even our own person once. In each and every instance, the eye of the beholder defines us.

This practice doesn't compromise individuals, it reconstitutes us as informational entities. It's a coding practice. The records of our individual lives are the flow of raw material for remaking us into probabilities designed to meet the purposes of others, and a probability as an informational entity has qualities of its own. It exists only when called up, can only be called up in particulars relative to the observer and when called up is open to entrance and manipulation. Based on us but not us, the profile is a post-human entity, half human and half machine.

This lens sets up and brings forth society in its own way, too, and that determines a second way in which the self is represented. The larger vision of society within which data-based marketing conceives its profiles is the geo-demo-psy-chographic segmentation schema. The multiple modifiers just mean that three different types of data—geographic, demographic and attitudinal—are used to parse the entire population into diverse lifestyle-based segments and to place each of us in the segment that we most resemble. Like tiles in a mosaic, however, the segments only make sense in the context of the whole.

The rarely discussed whole has three problematic features. First, it sees American society as a socio-economic stratification (SES) system. That way of understanding our social fabric is useful for marketers and the rest of us, but it's not the only way. Second, the vision of our SES system that's actually in use omits most of the socio-economic changes that occurred over the second half of the 20th century and actually challenge us today. Finally, like all feedback systems, this decision-making framework reinforces and perpetuates itself. In short, the self inside this machine is a set of probabilities useful to others, constantly changing but always tumbling in place.

Critics complain that our everyday life has become "informatized" and "interpenetrated by information flows" and that the self has become porous, "leaking out into the environment while open to entrance" and "multiplied by databases." Data-based marketing is the practice responsible in large part for these transformations. As a way of apprehending human affairs, it has, as its earliest critics feared, largely displaced people with probabilistic aggregates of ersatz "persons" and, applying Heidegger's definition of technology: it's one way we make our world ready for our consumption and make ourselves ready to consume it.

Cyber Personas

Cyberspace is also a pervasive computer-based technology that sets us up and brings us forth but in a different way. In the datascape, computers are used for crunching data and churning out probabilistic profiles; in cyberspace computers are used for communication. To understand how we're set up and brought forth in this machine world, it's first necessary to understand two basic facts about how cyberspace itself is set up. Specifically, the Web address and the hyperlink shape the Web into a terrain in which communications flows in certain directions. That's the context in which our cyber-persona is emerging.

Every Web page has a unique string of numbers, called a Universal Resource Locator (URL) that serves as its address. For human convenience, each numerical string is turned into a name (www.anysite.com) and can be extended into a name for a particular page on a particular site (www.anysite. com/sitemap). The International Corporation for Assigned Names and Numbers (ICANN) organizes all these addresses into one vast branching hierarchy. As one goes down the hierarchy, the branches get smaller and smaller until one gets to the one branch and then to the one leaf that's the precise Web page one is looking for. This hierarchy includes every site, every page, every image on the Web and is mandatory. For anything to appear on the Web, it must have an assigned name and number; if not, it doesn't exist. This tightly controlled, top-down hierarchy ensures that everything on the Web has one and only one location.

The hypertext link is a one-way pointer. Placed inside one URL (the source page), a link points to another URL (the destination page). Although any URL can link to any other URL, linking behavior follows a pattern: we insert links to those URLs that we know about and deem relevant.

That behavior is called preferential attachment and has consequences. The more inbound links a Web page gathers, the more others are likely to find it. Some will create new links to that page, making it likely that even more users will find that page; some of them in turn will create new links to that page, and so on. In short, the use of one-way links creates a popularity dynamic in which the well linked become even better linked.

Every network with stable nodes and one-way pointers evolves into a *directed* network with three "continents," and the Web is no exception. Applying the following map of a generic directed network to the Web, individuals are on the left, businesses on the right and search engines, portals and major online media are in the center. Individuals can create links that go in to the Central Core, a personal Web site,

The Continents of a Directed Network

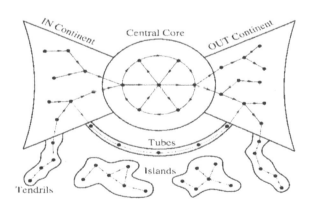

Source: Albert-László Barabási. *Linked: The New Science of Networks.* Cambridge, MA: Perseus Publishing, 2002.

for example, can link to a page at Yahoo or ESPN, but sites in the Core don't link back to individuals. From the Core, there are links going out to businesses and their brands but there are rarely any links going back; in fact, these nodes typically dead-end. (Individuals can and do sometimes link directly to business or brand sites but, again, they rarely link back.) According to a 2002 estimate, one can reach only 24 percent of the Web by following links.[8] Developments in the OUT and IN Continents are the contexts within which our cyberpersonas are emerging.

The book's second half explores our cyberpersona, and its leadoff chapter considers how we appear to the consumer-facing business sites of the OUT Continent. Most of us have visited this continent many times to book travel, buy a book, do our banking, shop for a car and conduct hundreds of other everyday consumer activities. From the marketer's perspective, our visits to their sites flow in an inbound direction. That's a new situation; traditionally, marketers communicate in an outbound direction. So, the buzz *du jour* along Madison Avenue is about less intrusion and more attraction, less capturing and more seducing, less talking and more listening. While marketers are busy inverting their practices, technical solutions are being developed that will take us to the logical conclusion: user-managed interfaces that enable each of us, through our ongoing and voluntary self-disclosure, to "advertise" our needs and wants as consumers to the vendors and merchants we hope will fulfill them   Such a role reversal would save marketers millions, but consumers aren't likely to get paid for making our needs and wants knowable. More likely, we'll think this empowering and freely invert ourselves from objects of marketers' desires into subjects to whom they can pay their attentions. This "virtual consumer" is a likely component of everyone's emerging cyberpersona.

Hundreds of millions of us are already busy happily disclosing ourselves, typing ourselves into public existence on the IN Continent via Web 2.0 services that enable users to generate content and connect with each other. The next chapter examines the most popular among today's services— social network sites, blogs, reviewer sites, file-hosting services and social bookmarking sites—to reveal how each service shapes our self-presentation in different and important ways and to suggest that cyberpersona has two components: content and connections. Content has two dimensions. One's online *presence* refers to the quantity of content one has generated, whereas one's online *reputation* refers to what others think of that content's quality. Our connections are the links to and from others with whom we share content, and our cyberpersona as a network phenomenon rests on, emerges from and expresses the patterns and rhythms of those connections: You are who you network with, where you link to and with whom you share. The two-fold process for generating "virtual me"—self-disclosure through content that creates presence and co-creation through connections (links and clicks) that create reputation—will likely become inescapable as more of our everyday life either occurs or is replicated online.

Cyberspace is setting us up and bringing us forth in a third way as well: enabling us to think together. Of course, no one ever thinks alone, but we rarely notice because the social basis for thinking resides in the deep background of consciousness, language and culture. The Web isn't changing that, but it is spawning several novel mechanisms that claim to generate and harness "collective intelligence," new knowledge that is greater than the sum of its inputs. These mechanisms are used behind the scenes at Google, Amazon, Netflix, eBay and other sites we know well. The last chapter examines closely the three most popular—crowdsourcing, recommender systems and prediction markets—to reveal what these mechanisms upload from our brains, how they process our inputs and whether the outputs they generate represent us in ways that are actually collective and intelligent.

The datascape and cyberspace are different machines and our simulacra—data profiles and cyberpersonas—are different. Both, however, are hybrids—part human, part machine. Our real lives are their raw materials, but we are brought forth in machine terms, as probabilities of behaviors and patterns of connections. In both machine worlds we become public, albeit in silicon rather than carbon, and although we cannot change how these machines set us up and bring us forth to and with others, the conclusion considers our rights and responsibilities to the post-human entities that re-present us inside these machines.

Two appendices provide practical advice for those who want to take up these matters in their personal lives: how to reduce commercial trafficking in one's personal information within the datascape and how to start building and managing one's self-presentation in cyberspace. In researching this book, I came across various satirical works that address its topics and gathered them into an interlude.

Notes

1 Sherwood Washburn, "Tools and Human Evolution," *Scientific American* 203 (September 1960), 63-75 is the classic statement.

2 This often-anthologized essay is included in Martin Heidegger, *Basic Writings*, ed. David Farrell Krell (New York: Harper & Row, 1977). Mark Poster, *What's the Matter with the Internet?* (Minneapolis: University of Minnesota Press, 2001) 27—38 provides a plain-English explanation.

3 Although the impersonal public and personal private spheres assert different claims on the individual, they are not opposed but complementary. Allan Silver, " 'Two Different Sorts of Commerce'—Friendship and Strangership in Civil Society," in Jeff Weintraub and Krishan Kumar, eds., *Public and Private in Thought and Practice: Perspectives on a Grand Dichotomy* (Chicago: University of Chicago Press, 1997), 43–74 suggests that making the public sphere impersonal created the opportunity for the private sphere to become personal.

4 Georg Simmel, "Individual and Society in Eighteenth- and Nine-teenth-Century Views of Life" in Kurt Wolff, trans. and ed., *The Sociology of Georg Simmel* (New York: The Free Press, 1967), 58-84.

5 Mark Poster, *The Mode of Information: Post-Structuralism and Social Context* (Chicago: University of Chicago Press, 1990) applies "postmodern" perspectives to different electronic media and provides much of the theoretical background used in this book.

6 This definition is a radically simplified version of the analysis offered by N. Katherine Hayles, *How We Became Post-Human: Virtual Bodies in Cybernetics, Literature and Informatics* (Chicago: The University of Chicago Press, 1999), especially 27-36. Others use the term to refer to a embodied entity that exceeds human skills and intellect through artificial intelligence, genetic engineering, brain-computer interfaces, psychopharmacology or other technologies. See, for example, Julian Pepperell, *The Posthuman Condition: Consciousness Beyond the Brain* (Bristol, UK: Intellect Ltd., 2003).

7 Alexander Solzenitsyn, *Cancer Ward* (New York: Farrar Straus and Giroux: 1999), 192.

8 Albert-László Barabási, *Linked: The New Science of Networks* (Cambridge, MA: Perseus Publishing, 2002). See also Duncan J. Watts, *Six Degrees: The Science of a Connected Age* (New York: W.W. Norton, 2003). It should be noted that "preferential attachment" occurs at every step down the Web's hierarchies, e.g., a multi-sports site has more links to better-linked sport-specific sites which have more links to better-linked team sites which have more links to better-linked player sites.

PART I

DATA PROFILES

CHAPTER I

FROM HUMAN NATURE TO NORMAL PEOPLE

We must improve our concrete experience of persons and things into ... general rules and principles but without being grounded in individual facts and feelings, we shall end as we began, in ignorance.

—William Hazlitt, *The Plain Speaker* (1826)

The efficiency of the great circuits—which we will soon enough all be hooked into and serving—is a direct function of their abstractness.

—Sven Birkerts, *The Gutenberg Elegies* (1994)

Francis Bacon's aphorism "Knowledge is power" also goes in the other direction: the powerful create knowledge. Just as important and hardly surprising, the knowledge they create serves their interests. Since Biblical times, for example, governments everywhere have taken censuses of their populations to determine who to tax and who to conscript, just as they made maps to determine what lands to tax and where to fight.[1] Social statistics is no different. It was born in the mid-17th century as a way to apprehend the new terrain of modernizing society, flourished from the mid-19th century onward as a tool in top-down social governance and is today the predominant lens through which governments and businesses conjure us up as citizens and consumers.[2]

This way of perceiving human affairs makes certain assumptions about the world. The discipline's pioneers proudly acknowledged them and championed the new type of knowledge they yielded while contemporary critics loudly disparaged its axioms as well as its outputs. Little has changed. The assumptions upon which the method is based were baked in at birth and still frame us today. This chapter is old news to those familiar with the history of number, but for others a quick look at social statistics' origins reveals what's gained and what's lost in this distinctively modern view of self and society.

In the medieval period, collective life and the individual's place in that life were based on hierarchal social relationships defined by birthright and custom, including royals and their courts, estates and their privileges, lords and their vassals, guilds and their members among others. These relationships were undermined as modernization brought in new ways of deploying capital and organizing trade, new concentrations of populations in cities and new arrangements of production, distribution and consumption. To help governments grasp this new social terrain, two competing schools of fact gathering emerged in the mid-17th century: university statistics and political arithmetic.

Strongest in Germany, university statistics was a way of describing the state by tabulating its people, land, wealth and all the other resources available to it. In contrast, political arithmetic, strongest in England, sought to understand the natural order: patterns in births, deaths, marriages and other regularities of human life. This difference in purpose reflected a difference in how the two schools of statistics viewed the relationship between individuals and society.

The university statistics perspective was holistic. In theory, community precedes the individual and is the context from within which individuals emerge. Similarly, in practice, this school argued that the true forces of the state—nationalism, the genius of the people, the love of freedom and others—could not be reduced to individuals or expressed in numerical form. Indeed, much of university statistics was non-quantitative.

Diametrically opposed, the political arithmetic perspective was atomistic. It found solid ground in individuals and aggregated them up into communities. Its first appearance was John Graunt's 1662 presentation to England's Royal Society on London's birth and death rates, an analysis undertaken with the hope of creating an early warning system against bubonic plague. Its philosophical origins appeared a bit earlier in Thomas Hobbes' 1651 *Leviathan*, the founding treatise of English political theory. Borrowing heavily from the new science of physics, Hobbes resolved society into its simplest elements, aggregated individuals. Then, using "principles" of human nature and "laws" of psychology, he composed those elements into a logical whole.[3] Of course, Hobbes' principles and laws reflected his view of his world and the result was bleak: man owes nothing to his fellow men. Worse, individuals are in constant rivalry with and in constant danger from each other, thus necessitating authoritarian rule by monarchs. We got out from under Hobbesian despotism, but it took another century of socio-economic modernization and corresponding philosophizing before John Locke could construct a liberal political philosophy on the basis of "enlightened" self-interest and Adam Smith could do the same for self-regulating markets in the economy. The founding assumption, that the individual precedes the community, was stronger than ever, and in the contest between the two schools of gathering and presenting social facts, political arithmetic prevailed.[4]

In the 19th century this way of apprehending society developed rapidly in two ways. Information gathering shifted from episodic projects to regular monitoring, and its scope expanded to include health, labor conditions, education, delinquency, crime and other "moral statistics" about the lower depths of the new society. It helped answer a need created by the triumph of Enlightenment politics. In the new modern society neither the monarchy, the aristocracy or the clergy had any privileges when making assertions about the world, for describing what is and what ought to be. Any project for society's reunification or even its tolerably harmonious governance needed a new basis of authority.

Into this vacuum stepped two new ways of apprehending the social world—ideology and the social sciences. Both were based on and appealed to reason, quite literally to the power of ideas as ways of seeing and thinking about the world for the tasks of mobilizing people and justifying collective action. Similarly, both relied on and championed the individual, newly released from customary social relationships, as the locus of power, not only for his capability but also for his moral responsibility to be rational. The ideologues focused on both what is and what ought to be, anchoring the latter in the former. The social sciences focused on what is but instead of what ought to be, they aimed more modestly for what could be better.[5] To the new social sciences, no method for apprehending collective life was more important than the new social statistics.

Ostensibly, this form of knowledge was objective. Its champions explicitly contrasted it to the traditional privileges of the elites to render their judgments in matters of social action, including how they measured things. In other words it was valued as much for its impartiality as for its truthfulness.[6] The aspiration to objectivity appeared prior to the birth of social statistics proper and continues to this day. The inventor of the calculus, binary code and much else, Gottfried Wilhelm Leibniz (1646—1716) hoped that one day all human disputes and questions of opinion would be solved by applied mathematics. Three centuries later, a leading champion of "the information society," sociologist Daniel Bell, would have the same aspiration: "These methods seek to substitute algorithms, that is, decision rules, for judgment."[7] The reality did not, however, always attain the objectivity that the new social statistics promised. Indeed, that problem—descriptions being (mis)used as evaluations—appeared at the very birth of this new discipline.

Technically, statistically "normal" means mathematically typical, but the 19th century moral reformers and social engineers, who pioneered the use of statistics in public health, sanitation, education, penology and other areas, were all too prone to turn what is into what ought to be. Adolphe Quetelet, a leading 19th century champion of social statistics and inventor of *l'homme moyen*—the average man—illustrates how easily the normal became the normative:

> Average man, provided he was absolutely defined, could be … regarded as the model of beauty; whereas more significant deviations from his proportions, his faculties and abilities belonged to the realm of malformations and diseases; whatever was not just dissimilar to these proportions and forms but went beyond these observed extremes would have to be regarded as a monstrosity.[8]

The normal was good and the farther from normal one was, the more deviant one was. Thus, statistical normality and abnormality provided the "scientifically objective" rationale for the new social scientists to classify people as healthy or diseased, sane or insane, adjusted or alienated and so forth. They then prescribed, in some cases imposed, various reforming and improving regimes on those population segments that they found along the tails of their frequency distributions and in the "wrong" boxes of their classification schemes.[9]

Social scientists weren't the only ones who turned is into ought. Ideologues did as well. Those on the left did so explicitly while those on the right did so somewhat covertly. Political conservatives, for example, equated the statistically typical with what is normatively right, creating a self-fulfilling justification for the status quo. Cultural elitists applied a different twist: they saw the statistically normal as mediocrity, thus rationalizing their style of top-down efforts at improvement. Whether explicit or implicit, whether by ideologues or social scientists, whether from the left or the right, whether yesterday or today, the turning of descriptions into evaluations is a superficial problem; it resides in how statistics are used. The root-level problem with social statistics was, and remains, the assumption that facts and values are separable.

Some asserted that the values that motivate humans— our ideals, aspirations and possibilities—are not observable as facts and excluded them. Others asserted that facts about us—our health, longevity, literacy and welfare—could be apprehended without regard to values and excluded them that way. Either way, social statistics makes the utilitarian promise to treat people as things. Of course, people are things, embodied entities in time and space, just like every-thing else in the carbon-based world. Our materiality is a matter of fact. It was and remains the particular promise of social statistics, however, to treat humans as things and only as things, achieved largely by bracketing off our qualities as unknowable and thus outside the domain of its quantitative analysis.

That is the root-level limitation in how the lens of sta-tistics apprehends humans: much of what's most impor-tant to us, indeed what distinguishes us as human, is pre-scinded as unmeasurable. That, too, was apparent early on; indeed it was part of the rationale for creating the new discipline. Although social statistics saw the individual as the irreducible unit of society and represented the human experience as individuated, it could not, and still cannot, say anything about individuals. Individuals were, and re-main, too variable and inconsistent, too complex and di-verse to be the basis for any science of the social condition. The very raison d'etre for creating social statistics was to provide an alternative. Although the individual could not be predicted or even understood, Quetelet's *l'homme moyen* could be.

A rave review of Quetelet's work, by astronomer John Herschel, made explicit all four elements of the new *social* statistics: its aspiration to govern human affairs, its reliance on the model of the physical sciences, its inability to measure what cannot be observed and the categorically social phe-nomenon that it could measure:

Statistics ... affords the only secure ground on which the truth or falsehood of the theories and hypotheses of that complicated science can be brought to the test. It is not unadvisedly that we use the term Dynamics as applied to the mechanism and movements of the social body, nor is it by any loose metaphor or strained analogy that much of the language of mechanical philosophy finds a parallel meaning in the discussion of such subjects ...

Number, weight, and measure are the foundations of all exact science; neither can any branch of human knowledge be held advanced which does not, in some way or other, frame its theories or correct its practice by reference to these elements.

What astronomical records or meteorological registers are to a rational explanation of the movements of the planets or of the atmosphere, statistical returns are to social and political philosophy. They assign, at determinate intervals, the numerical values of the variables which form the subject matter of its reasonings, or at least of such functions of them as are accessible to direct observation, which it is the business of sound theory so to analyze or combine as to educe from them those deeper-seated elements which enter into the expression of general laws.[10]

In other words, social statistics breaks down the social body into elements that can be numbered, weighed and measured and then proceeds to observe and capture our numerical values on those variables. It sees society as an aggregate of individuals but what it measures is individual *variability*, one observed value per individual along some yardstick of a common attribute. Advanced statistical procedures can turn descriptions into predictions, but again, the method predicts frequencies of behavior among a population of individuals. It can neither explain nor predict behaviors of individuals.

Quite the opposite, the technique of aggregating individuals brackets all the factors—motive, volition, knowledge and intent—that might actually explain, rather than just measure, the individual instance of the behavior under scrutiny.

Privileging measurement over understanding, social statistics did not sit well with two founding fathers of sociology. Auguste Comte (1798—1857) argued that human development follows three paths forward—theological, metaphysical and scientific. Social statistics, by slicing and dicing the human experience, just makes a muddle of what he thought most important in understanding what moves humans.

The criticism by Frédéric Le Play (1806—1882) was even more pointed. An avid quantifier but an ardent opponent of statistics, Le Play's chef d'oeuvre, the six-volume *Les Ouvriers Europeans (European Workers)* scrutinized the household budgets of 36 representative working-class families across Europe. Following an older analytic tradition, he mixed his quantitative approach with qualitative elements: historical insights, singular facts and considered judgments. Here and elsewhere, he argued that one could learn from representative individuals more about the larger class they represented than from statistics because carefully chosen cases reveal better than mechanistic tabulations how people's needs, pleasures and, most important, their possibilities motivate them.

At the turn of the 20th century, the noted economist Alfred Marshall acknowledged the superiority of le Play's method over a purely statistical view for yielding insights about what actually moved individual consumers but also emphasized that the method required an analyst with le Play's talents. Unfortunately, the analysts working in government and business were "ordinary hands," and if they were to use such an approach, they would likely draw untrustworthy conclusions. A purely statistical view was less insightful but safer:

> It may be noted that the method of Le Play's monumental *Les Ouvriers Europeans* is the *intensive* study of all the details of the domestic life of a few care-

fully chosen families. To work it well requires a rare combination of judgment in selecting cases, of insight and sympathy in interpreting them. At its best, it is the best of all: but in ordinary hands it is likely to suggest more untrustworthy general conclusions than those obtained by the extensive method of collecting more rapidly very numerous observations, reducing them as far as possible to statistical form, and obtaining broad averages in which inaccuracies and idiosyncrasies may be trusted to counteract one another to some extent.[11]

In the 1920s, when the social research community tried to fill this insight gap by turning to the statistical study of attitudes, the same quantitative technique was used with the same results. Researchers isolated and extracted from their contexts various hopes and fears, laid each out on a linear scale or bipolar continuum, located individuals on such axes and counted up our variability on the attitude. Once again, statistical procedures delivered frequencies and percentages within populations but couldn't explain individuals.[12]

This didn't satisfy marketers, and in the 1940s they and their advertising agencies turned to qualitative research, initially to psychoanalytically inspired motivational research and later to techniques such as focus groups and one-on-one interviews, to get beyond measurement to explanation. The goal of such research methods is not to project findings from a sample onto an entire population but to gain from representative individuals insights about their goals and aspirations, exactly le Play's position a century earlier. The limitation of marketing data, the commercial cousin of social statistics, was reprised in Nicholas Samstag's 1966 essay for *Madison Avenue* magazine, "You Can't Make a Good Advertisement Out of Statistics" and again in 1980 by consumer researcher Morris Holbrook, who mocked the achievements of the data-based approach for its ability to capture everything except what's actually important to us:

Yes, we can build multi-attribute models that predict preference toward toothpaste; we can generate
complex multidimensional spaces that represent
perceptions of cigarettes; we can construct devilish-
ly clever procedures that trace the acquisition of information on cereal brands; we can—with our bare
hands—construct mighty regression analyses that
relate detergent usage to 300 life-style variables. In
short—when it comes to the factors of least importance to the consumer's emotional, cultural and
spiritual existence—we excel.[13]

Today, both advertising and data-based marketing rely
on representative individuals from whom explanations may
be acquired as to why consumers may buy, because marketing data cannot get there.

The limitation in using data to apprehend human affairs, then and now, reflects in large part the nature of all
data and how all data are constructed. This is the problem
of abstraction; that is, creating data about *any* reality requires
performing radical surgery on that reality. The procedure
for making a datum goes like this:

1. Isolate one particular feature embedded in a larger situation. Then, extract the feature by throwing away the larger
   situation.
2. Redefine the feature as a variable, the current status of
   which can be observed as a numerical value.
3. Observe an instance of the variable and record its current
   value at that moment. .

In short, isolate and extract, redefine and freeze is how a
datum is born.

Yale computer scientist David Gelernter, a chief champion of using data and computerized databases to create a
"mirror world" of real life, acknowledges but only in pass-
ing what this process tosses aside. The creation of every

data model, he writes, "seeks to identify and extract, that is, abstract from the rich and complex interrelationships among entities in the real world, those quantifiable attributes which if managed correctly promise to bring order and structure to that world, omitting whole tangles of facts and perceptions that never get sorted out."[14] For Gelernter order and structure are the primary goals and are achieved by ignoring the jumbled tangles of human actuality.

No one can question the value of creating data about the world. Our species' ability to arrange things in rows and columns predates our invention of numbers,[15] and after their invention, human life has required and progressed by counting, measuring and calculating. Data is knowledge in a form that can be combined or divided, compared and contrasted to broaden or narrow the scope over which its possessors assert knowledge, make decisions and achieve impact. Civilization could not exist if we hadn't cut up the world into manipulatable units and that includes human affairs.

Around the time Francis Bacon said that knowledge is power, his contemporary Galileo Galilei said, "Nature is written in the language of mathematics." It's not likely he meant to include human nature, but that aspiration soon appeared in the works of G. W. Leibniz. The 17th century German polymath knew well that the process of abstraction cannot be applied everywhere. He made the point with quiet precision in "The Method of Mathematics" in the *Preface to the General Science:*

> An ancient saying has it that God created everything according to weight, measure, and number. However, there are many things which cannot be weighed, whatever is not effected by force or power, and anything which is not divisible into parts escapes measurement.

In the very next sentence, however, he revealed the seductive appeal of number as such to those who would master the universe:

> On the other hand, there is nothing which is not
> subsumable under number. Number is therefore,
> so to speak, a fundamental metaphysical form, and
> arithmetic a sort of statics of the universe, in which
> the powers of things are revealed.

Indeed, he was quite wrapped up in a Faustian ambition to create an algebra of human thought that could understand, resolve and govern human affairs:

> It is obvious that if we could find characters or signs
> suited for expressing all our thoughts as clearly and
> as exactly as arithmetic expresses numbers or ge-
> ometry expresses lines, we could do in all matters
> *insofar as they are subject to reasoning* all that we can
> do in arithmetic and geometry. For all investiga-
> tions which depend on reasoning would be carried
> out by transposing these characters and by a species
> of calculus.[16]

Despite his skill at devising notational systems, Leibniz didn't make any progress on that score. Nor has anyone since then figured out a way in which data will free us from the responsibility of judgment or, as Daniel Bell hopes, put an end to ideology and other contestations. The language of mathematics is sufficient for measuring nature because phe-nomena like heat, speed and gravity don't have hopes and dreams, but when applied to human affairs, as in social sta-tistics and its descendants, there's just too much about what makes us tick that is not "subject to reasoning" and that data cannot capture.

Specifically, data cannot capture our qualities or our possibilities. Isaiah Berlin was among many philosophers who argued that our "purposes, motives, acts of will, deci-sions, doubts, hesitations, thoughts, hopes, fears, desires and so forth...are among the ways that we distinguish human be-ings from the rest of nature." Ernst Bloch was among many philosophers who argued that the observable is not our only reality "The presence which is usually called reality," he wrote, " is surrounded by a tremendously greater ocean of objectively real possibility … We live surrounded by possibility, not merely by presence. In the prison of mere presence we could not even move nor even breathe." An anonymous versifier combined both limitations in a simple analogy:

> In modern thought (if not in fact)
> Nothing is that doesn't act.
> So that is reckoned wisdom which
> Describes the scratch but not the itch.[17]

Counting how often we scratch is essential to human life, but however precise and predictive our counting, it doesn't explain the itch. The itch is what we omit when we turn away from the unmeasurables of human nature and focus on counting how often we scratch.

It is easy to overstate the power of data. The 20th century economist Joseph Schumpeter, for example, saw our increasingly quantitative habits of mind, once established in and by the economy, commence "upon a conqueror's career subjugating—rationalizing—man's tools and philosophies, his medical practice, his picture of the cosmos, his outlook on life, everything in fact including his concepts of beauty and justice and his spiritual ambitions."[18] Schumpeter and others credit data with capabilities it doesn't have. The concepts and ambitions that have impelled and enabled humankind, individually and collectively, to give our lives meaningful direction cannot be stated exactly and cannot be captured as data. As data becomes the predominant lens for understanding and action in human affairs, it doesn't so much subjugate or rationalize; it just pushes off the stage those cultural traditions that do express our qualities and our possibilities.[19] It's a surreptitious coercion into cultural amnesia.

Certainly, our qualities and possibilities don't come with us as we assimilate into the datascape. In the great circuits we are integrated as always-on transceivers in a continuous two-way flow of data that feeds a pervasive system of reciprocally governing humans and machines that informs decision making about the made and natural environments in which we live. The vision of Joel de Rosney is typical:

> This hybrid life, at once biological, mechanical and electronic, is still coming into being before our very eyes. And we are its cells. In a still unconscious way, we are contributing to the invention of its metabolism, its circulation and its nervous system. We call them economies, markets, roads, communications, networks and electronic highways, but they are the organs and vital systems of an emerging super-organism.[20]

Constructing human affairs in terms a machine can read has proven hugely effective in optimizing the status quo, always yielding something a little bit better over the course of time, and without question this data-based leviathan will continue to increase our efficiency and effectiveness in instrumental action. But whatever is pulsing along these circuits doesn't include much of what counts most to humans.

Alfred North Whitehead warned against "the taking as real of something, whether a physical thing or a scientific conception, that has been abstracted from reality for special purposes of thought,"[21] and it applies here, to the hypothetical "persons" populating the datascape. Reducing ourselves into versions that a machine can read explains why the outcomes of this crunching and processing don't and can't satisfy us at certain levels: ersatz versions of us go in, and ersatz answers about us come out. At the same time, the ersatz inputs and outputs still advance the commercial and administrative purposes of those who built, own and operate the apparatus.

Although these limitations of social statistics were baked in at birth, this way of apprehending human affairs took on the large-scale proportions of a technology in the Heideggerian sense in the 1970s when marketing, the function responsible for managing the demand side of supply and demand, embraced the use of data on a broad scale and with ever-greater sophistication. The enabling factors were the rapid drop in the price of computing processing power for businesses and the availability of machine-readable household- and individual-level data. But the cause was an epochal shift in the economy to which we now turn.

Notes

1 The first half of Otis Dudley Duncan, *Notes on Social Measurement: Historical and Critical* (New York: Russell Sage Foundation, 1984) is an easy, almost breezy history of social measurement from Homer and Herodotus to the modern period. Harold Innis, *The Bias of Communication* (Toronto: University of Toronto Press, 1951) explores the role of data collection in "territorial management" in early civilizations; Armand Mattelart, *The Invention of Communication* (Minneapolis: University of Minnesota Press, 1996) does the same for France, Germany and England in the 19th and 20th centuries.

2 For histories of statistics and probability, none are better than Ian Hacking, *The Emergence of Probability: A Philosophical Study of Early Ideas about Probability, Induction and Statistical Inference* (Cambridge, UK: Cambridge University Press, 1975) and *The Taming of Chance* (New York: Cambridge University Press, 1990).

3 J.W.N. Watkins, "Philosophy and Politics in Hobbes," *Philosophical Quarterly*, vol. v (1959), 125—146 explains Hobbes' reliance on the physical sciences.

4 In the United States, political arithmetic triumphed with the seventh federal census of 1850. For the first time, statistics on the nation were reported not by families but by individuals and went

beyond enumeration to include facts on social and economic life: on agriculture and industry, schools and colleges, churches, libraries, newspapers, pauperism, crime and wages. To put this in context, James Madison had been rebuffed for even suggesting that the 1790 census document the differences among the country's agricultural, commercial and manufacturing interests. See Patricia Cline Cohen, *A Calculating People: The Spread of Numeracy in Early America* (New York: Routledge, 1999), 159—164.

5 Alvin W. Gouldner, *The Dialectic of Ideology and Technology: The Origins, Grammar and Future of Ideology* (New York: Oxford University Press, 1982), 23—67 compares social science and ideology as new ways of apprehending the world and mobilizing action that emerged in the 19th century.

6 Witold Kula, *Measures and Men* (Princeton: Princeton University Press, 1986) recounts how elites measured things before measurement was standardized. Theodore M. Porter, "Objectivity as Standardization: The Rhetoric of Impersonality in Measurement, Statistics and Cost-Benefit Analysis" in Allan Megill, ed. *Rethinking Objectivity* (Durham, NC: Duke University Press, 1994), 197—238, especially 206—210, explains the new "fairness."

7 Daniel Bell, "The Social Framework of the Information Society," in Michael I. Dertouzos and Joel Moses, eds., *The Computer Age: A Twenty-Year View* (Cambridge, MA: MIT Press, 1979), 167.

8 Quoted in Wofgang Pircher, "Tours Through the Back-Country of Imperfectly Informed Society" in Jennifer Daryl Slack and Fred Fejes, eds., *The Ideology of the Information Age* (Norwood, NJ: Ablex Publishing Company, 1987), 69.

9 The perils in applying classification schemes to people are explored in Ian Hacking, "Making People Up," in Thomas C. Heller et al., eds., *Reconstructing Individualism: Autonomy, Individuality and the Self in Western Thought* (Stanford: Stanford University Press, 1986), 222—236 and Geoffrey C. Bowker and Susan Leigh Starr,

Sorting Things Out: Classification and Its Consequences (Cambridge, MA: The MIT Press, 1999).

10 Quoted in Duncan, 97.

11 Alfred Marshall, *Principles of Economics* [1890] (London: Macmillan, 1920), 116.

12 Gard Gigerenzer et al., *The Empire of Chance: How Probability Changed Science and Everyday Life* (Cambridge, UK: Cambridge University Press, 1989), 251—255 and Donald Fleming, "Attitude: The History of a Concept," *Perspectives in American History* 1 (1967), 287—265 explore the efforts to quantify attitudes. Duncan, 172—176, reviews the technical challenges, the most important of which persist to this day.

13 Morris B. Holbrook, "Introduction: The Esthetic Imperative in Consumer Research," in Elizabeth C. Hirschman and Morris B. Holbrook, eds., *Symbolic Consumer Behavior* (Ann Arbor: Association for Consumer Research, 1980), 36. Jan S. Slater, "Qualitative Research in Advertising" in John Philip Jones, ed., *How Advertising Works: The Role of Research* (Thousand Oaks, CA: Sage Publications, 1988), 121—135 explains the role and offers a good review of qualitative research techniques.

14 David Gelertner, *Mirror Worlds: or the Day Software Puts the Universe in a Shoebox... How It Will Happen and What It Will Mean* (New York: Oxford University Press, 1991). It's worth noting that data can measure but not explain change either. A datum is created when a variable is observed and its present status recorded as a value, but there's nothing in-between the points of data that explains the change in status from one moment to the next.

15 Jack Goody, *The Domestication of the Savage Mind* (London: Cambridge University Press, 1978), 52—112.

16 G.W. Leibniz, "The Method of Mathematics" in Roger Bishop Jones, trans., *Preface to the General Science*, www.rbjones.com/rbj-pub/philos/classics/leibniz/meth_math.htm.

17 Isaiah Berlin, *Vico & Herder: Two Studies in the History of Ideas* (New York: Vintage, 1977) 22; Ernst Bloch, "Man (sic) as Possibility," *Cross Currents*, vol. 18 (1968), 273—283. The source of the anonymous quatrain is Marshall McLuhan, *Understanding Media: The Extensions of Man* (New York: McGraw-Hill, 1964), 25.

18 Joseph Schumpeter, *Capitalism, Socialism and Democracy* (New York: Harper & Row, 1942), 124.

19 The classic statement of this concern by a computer scientist is Joseph Weizenbaum, *Computer Power and Human Reason: From Judgment to Calculation* (San Francisco: W.H. Freeman & Company, 1976).

20 Joel de Rosnay, *The Symbiotic Man: A New Understanding of the Organization of Life and a Vision of the Future* (New York: McGraw-Hill, 2000), xxii—xxiii.

21 Alfred North Whitehead, *Science and the Modern World* (New York: Macmillan, 1925), 79.

CHAPTER 2

BEING DIFFERENT
FROM THE JONESES

We are just statistics, born to consume resources.

—Horace, *Epistles* I.2

For every man alone thinks he hath got
To be a Phoenix, and that then can be
None of that kind which he is but he.

—John Donne, *First Anniversarie* (1611)

Quaker Oats cereal, Ivory soap, Nabisco crackers and many other consumer goods we know well were introduced to American households during the last decades of the 19th century. They were products of the Industrial Revolution, a transformation in the use of energy that yielded mechanized factories, the railroad grid and telegraphy. They became national brands with the advent of mass media. That milestone is usually marked by the passage of the Postal Act of 1879, which gave magazines low-cost mailing privileges, but its business model took a while longer to gel. In 1893, Frank Munsey realized that reducing the price of *Munsey's Magazine* to below cost would attract a much larger circulation, which in turn would attract much more advertiser spending. He figured correctly: the increased advertiser revenue far exceeded the decreased reader revenue and generated large profits. And that's how advertising-supported mass media was born.

Data-based marketing was also born in a "revolution" – the harnessing of information to production, to transportation and to communication in the 1970s. Of course, businesses had collected research data from the marketplace for decades with such tools as magazine questionnaires (1914), opinion surveys (1929) and audience measurement services (1935). Indeed, the first cybernetic system appeared as far back as 1924. Alfred Sloan, General Motors' (GM's) manager of parts and accessories who would later become CEO, set up system in which sales volumes were collected from GM dealers every 10 days and then used to govern parts purchasing and production volumes at its factories. Following Sloan's innovation, "control" systems that used continuous feedback from the marketplace grew in number and sophistication.[1]

In the 1970s two technological changes occurred and in combination enabled the broad diffusion of data-based decision making among consumer businesses. One was the new abundance of consumer-level purchase data, thanks to the application of bar codes on products, the use of credit cards for everyday purchases and the popularity of frequent-shopper programs at retail. At the same time information about consumers' households became available, thanks to the federal government's release of census data in machine-readable form. The other change was the democratization of data processing. Thanks to the invention of the micro-processor and to the separation of hardware and software, the computing power that once required a mainframe was compressed into workstations for technical professions and then packed into desktop machines that all business functions could use.

Abundant data and low cost data processing were elements of the larger "Information Revolution" of the 1970s. While the Industrial Revolution had harnessed energy in new ways to create economic value, the Information Revolution harnessed computing and communication in new ways to create economic value. There's a lively academic debate about whether the Information Revolution was a real break or just a phase in the history of capitalism, about whether or not we had actually shifted from an industrial to a post-industrial economy.[2] Either way, in the last decades of the 20th century, businesses began reorganizing their productive assets, moving away from fixed arrangements that had been developed to harness energy and toward flexible arrange-ments that could harness the power of information.[3]

As a new way for business to create value, information technologies were applied to all business functions, starting upstream with new product research and continuing through design, pricing, manufacture, distribution and culminating with sales and marketing. From the outside, that is, from the consumer's view, the economy shifted from mass manu-facturing and mass marketing the one-size-fits-all American Dream to the manufacturing of variety and the marketing of difference. This change was profound for both supply and demand sides, and it took a crisis in the prevailing business paradigm to bring it about.

The Prevailing Paradigm

Since the last decades of the 19th century, the economy's success in producing and distributing uniform products for nationwide sale rested on businesses' success in maximizing control over their own productive resources. To do so, that era's "captains of industry" and "robber barons" (depending on one's point of view) integrated their companies in two ways. The vertically integrated company gathered under uni-fied ownership all the different steps in its process, from the raw materials that went into its products to the transportation systems that moved both raw materials and finished goods and even in some cases to the outfits that sold them. The Carnegie Steel Co., for example, owned not only steel mills but also the mines that provided the iron and coal from which steel is made, the ships and railroads that transported these raw materials to the factory, the furnaces that turned coal into coke and so on. The horizontally integrated company tried to own just one thing but everywhere. The railroads, for example, consolidated successfully and rather notoriously in this era while American Telephone and Telegraph (AT&T) achieved its monopoly on long-distance calling. The most famous conglomerate of all, John D. Rockefeller's Standard Oil, achieved its dominance by combining vertical and horizontal integration. Although Progressive reformers busted up many trusts, cartels and combines in the early 20th century, the business efficiency of integrating productive assets into fixed arrangements was an unqualified success.

But success also brought its own problem: the economy's supply side could produce automobiles, vacuum cleaners and other consumer durables in great volumes but the demand side could not absorb them. Henry Ford devised a solution. In 1914 at the just-completed Ford factory in Dearborn, Michigan, he introduced the $5, eight-hour workday. More than a payoff to secure workers' compliance with the discipline of the assembly line, it reflected Ford's novel belief that mass production required mass consumption. That is, $5 for eight hours of work would provide wages that actually allowed for the purchase of these products as well as the leisure hours that allowed for their use. Fordism redefined the relationship between labor and capital as a win-win virtuous circle and sank firm roots as a model for the future. It had not yet spread widely or deeply, however, when the stock market crashed in 1929 and national economies, here and elsewhere, slid into the Great Depression of the 1930s.

One response to this crisis, followed by Japan, Italy and Germany, was fascism with its appeals to mythology, militarism and racism. The other, championed by the British economist John Maynard Keynes and followed by the United Kingdom and United States, was to provide government support for Fordism, mostly along three dimensions:

o   Expenditures on infrastructure such as transportation and energy that were vital to the growth of mass production and mass consumption and also created jobs

o   Expenditures to support a "social wage" in such areas as education, health care, housing and retirement benefits
o   Intervention if necessary to affect wage agreements and protect workers' rights

These policies helped but did not cure. The U.S. economy only came around with the ramped up production of armaments and materiel for World War II. In Europe and Japan the Fordist-Keynsian solution took hold after the war. It was required by the Allies' occupation policies, subsidized by the Marshall Plan and exported via direct investment by U.S. corporations in those regions.

From the close of the war through the 1960s, the Fordist-Keynsian paradigm prevailed, not everywhere and not for everyone, but broadly. Mass consumption supported mass production, which supported full employment, which supported mass consumption in a virtuous cycle. By the mid-1960s, the economies of the United States, Western Europe and Japan were prosperous in their home markets and turned to creating export markets. That move, however, brought new rivals and fiercer rivalries into the home markets of each.

Economic affairs went from bad to worse after the 1971 Bretton Woods agreement took the U.S. dollar off the gold standard. No longer fixed to bullion, exchange rates floated and the dollar devalued. Within a few years, inflation rose to an annualized rate of 10 percent, and unemployment also rose to 10 percent while the gross national product slumped almost 5 percent annually. Then, came the "energy crisis" of 1973—1974. It began when oil-producing Arab nations decided to boycott Israel and its allies and intensified a year later when they ended their boycott but more than doubled the price of oil. In other categories, deflating prices prevailed from 1973—1975 along with persistently high unemployment and idle factories. The business solution followed in the United States was to dismantle the Fordist-Keynsian approach with its interlocking arrangements between big business, big labor and big government and to pursue a new flexibility in how productive resources were organized.

The Manufacture of Variety

Labor, already sapped by unemployment levels unmatched in the postwar era, weakened further when some of the country's biggest employers started outsourcing production to developing nations, where wages were lower. Then, a wave of "right sizing," enabled on the factory floor by process reengineering and automation, permanently reduced headcounts even further. Finally, unions work rules, job definitions, seniority requirements and the like were inimical to the flexibility that business now wanted, and the unions themselves were vigorously attacked. On the job the new requirement on all labor everywhere was flexibility, euphemistically called multi-skilling and continuous learning.

Nor was the new flexibility limited to factory jobs. White-collar work also changed. Top-down, centrally managed bureaucracies of 'organization men" were increasingly supplanted by flexible, horizontal arrangements in which

> Highly trained employees ... take on greater autonomy, being self-starting and self-motivating, moving from place to place, task to task, with great speed and fluidity. "Ad-hocracy" would rule, with groups of people spontaneously knitting together across organization lines, tackling the problems at hand, applying intense computer-aided expertise to it, and then vanishing whence they came.[4]

Businesses even started backing away from full-time employment and relying instead on part-time, temporary and subcontracted arrangements. (That's still going. Now that we are connected to the information superhighway, each of us can work in our own electronic cottage, facilitated by new time arrangements—flex time, part time and over time—as all labor becomes an always-on, on-demand resource.) Most telling, businesses' search for flexibility was not limited to labor but extended to how it organized its other productive assets. The integrated enterprise was partially dismantled by the same movement to outsource as many tasks in the enterprise value chain as possible. Moreover, following lessons learned from Japanese heavy industry, manufacturing reorganized its materials-handling and fabrication processes. "Total Quality Management," the simultaneous pursuit of improved quality and lower costs, led to product designs that were simpler to manufacture; just-in-time inventory practices made raw materials available exactly when needed while new factory layouts for agile manufacturing enabled small-batch production runs. These and other new manufacturing processes had two overall consequences on the marketplace's supply side: an acceleration in the rate of product innovation and the proliferation of differentiated products high in design intensity and symbolic content, produced in low volumes that could be sold at high margins to smaller market segments. In short, the supply side had reorganized to provide not only the new and improved but also the different and with ever-increasing diversity. Marketing, the business function responsible for aligning the demand side with the supply side, undertook a similar shift in the 1970s.

The Marketing of Difference

For most of the 20th century, consumer marketing relied on advertising in mass media to reach mass markets. For the most part it portrayed the benefits of the county's prosperity as improving material conditions for all Of course, there were rich and poor, but the American Dream applied to everyone and most advertising sold products in that context.[5] Interrupted by the Great Depression and World War II but resumed with new vigor thereafter, this consensus on the good life became the conformity of the Eisenhower years and took a nasty turn when Sen. Joseph McCarthy and other Cold Warriors began hunting down Commies, pinkos and fellow travelers, real and imagined, in Washington, Hollywood and elsewhere. Around the same time, critics started complaining that the American Dream had become a one-size-fits-all straightjacket. Sociologists worried that America had become a lonely crowd of organization men and status seekers while psychologists became less concerned with the psycho-sexual concepts of id, ego and super-ego and more concerned with psycho-social concepts of identity, roles and the presentation of self to others.[6]

The 1960s brought an end to the culture of conformity. The first crack came under the pressure of the Vietnam War. It is generally forgotten that the initial response to anti-war opposition was to deny its legitimacy. "America: Love It or Leave It" was no doubt an extreme sentiment, but "My Country, Right or Wrong" was a credible position for many, even if it did tend to abrogate our freedoms of speech, the press and assembly. Liberals who supported the war couldn't go that far. They argued instead that only the government had all the facts and denied legitimacy to anti-war critics that way. When draft boards began inducting the children of the middle class, anti-war sentiment erupted into increasingly frequent and popular protests, and the arguments that would deny legitimacy to dissent crumbled. Indeed, one lasting contribution of the 1960s was to restore the legitimacy of dissent.

The other was to legitimate difference. At first, black people wanted equality but then expanded their scope to include black pride; they would have not only their rights as citizens but also their responsibilities to each other as members of a race-based community Feminists were one small step behind but followed the same trajectory—from the rights-based claim to "Equal Pay for Equal Work" to the sex-based best seller *Our Bodies, Our Selves.* Hispanic Americans, Native Americans and gays and lesbians, all wanted the same: equal rights and the right to be different. By the 1970s the old idea of America as a "melting pot" in which different cultural identities were dissolved was replaced by the notion of a national mosaic in which such differences would be respected and preserved.

Although advertising agencies were quick to co-opt and sanitize the counter-culture of hipsters and hippies,[7] marketing as a whole began a much larger transformation in the 1970s, its turn to variety. Enabled by the new flexibility on the economy's supply side, the demand side, both consumers and the marketers who addressed them, shifted from keeping up with the Joneses to being different from them, from living within a common culture to crafting diverse lifestyles from an ever-faster flood of fashion and innovation, ideas and values. In other words "different" from the supply side required a demand side that was heterogeneous, for which the slicing and dicing of data-based marketing would be the enabling technologies.

The cybernetic potential of the Information Age was already apparent. One booster saw a day coming when the wired household would be the ultimate feedback loop and bring information's potential for marketing to fruition:

> The return channel in interactive systems … will transmit back to industry much relevant information about consumer demand and consumption. The information will include the consumer's identity, the time and place of consumption … and product characteristics. This data … will generate an invaluable portrait of consumer activity for marketing purposes. These systems will create a truly cybernetic cycle of production and consumption; because every consumptive activity will generate information pertinent to the modification of future production.[8]

The vision was right but the reality was messy. Rather than a steady stream of tidy packets about the Smiths and another about the Joneses, marketers got a deluge of disparate data about everyone from everywhere.

This challenge was solved by another economic feature of the Information Revolution sweeping through economy: the emergence of a new occupational stratum of knowledge workers. Throughout the decade leading thinkers from many disciplines, including economist John Kenneth Galbraith, sociologist Daniel Bell, futurist Alvin Toffler and management consultant Peter F. Drucker to name just a few, drew attention to the increasing number and diversity of those who created, fed and managed the new post-Fordist flexibility through data sciences and the symbolic arts.[9]

In short, as the supply side grew capable of manufacturing variety, marketing shifted to the cultivation of difference to foster a heterogeneous demand side. Data was plentiful, data processing was cheap and data analysts were at hand. The transformation of direct mail marketing and its explosive growth in the 1970s and 1980s are the most visible manifestations of this shift.

Direct mail marketing was born in 1884 with the first mail-order catalog from the company that would become Sears, Roebuck, and, ever since, catalog-based "retailing at a distance" has been a good business. Two events in the 1970s enabled the direct mail to become data-based marketing: the U.S. Postal Service's introduction of five-digit zip codes and the U.S. Census Bureau's release of household-level data in machine-readable form. Now that postal geographies could be described in terms of the attributes of the households within them, they could be sorted based on those attributes and then mailed.

The first geographic segmentation system for the United States, PRIZM from Claritas Inc. launched in 1974, and the direct marketing business grew rapidly thereafter. In 1975 there were roughly 300 commercial databases; 10 years later, there were over 2,000. Subscribers to these data services numbered 5,000 in 1975; within 10 years, they numbered 675,000. National business media reported that marketers were poised to pounce on the 1980 U.S. census upon its release, as were the rapidly growing number of agencies specializing in database marketing.[10]

Catalogers like L.L. Bean and subscription businesses like Columbia House took to the new data-based marketing first. For decades L. L. Bean had mailed two catalogs, in spring and fall. In this decade it began segmenting its customer lists and unbundling its catalogs into multiple versions; some segments got as many as 12 catalogs, others as few as 4. In the 1980s all sorts of businesses jumped in, notably airlines, phone companies, banks, automobile manufacturers, oil companies and department stores. Databases got more precise, too, shifting from zip codes, which typically contain 6,000 households, to census tracks, which typically contain 1,500 households, then downsizing to census subtracts and to nine-digit zips that contain as few as 10 households. Data processing costs also plummeted at this time. A name and postal address typically contain 1,000 bits of data. To process those bits in 1973 cost over $7; in 1987, it cost one penny.[11] A new magazine *American Demographics* hit the newsstands, the first college curriculum in direct marketing was offered at the University of Missouri, Kansas City in 1984, and throughout the decade a spate of how-to business books, including one that promised to help executives become "information confident" by raising their "information consciousness," proclaimed a revolutionary new marketing science.[12]

The concurrent growth in direct mail, the preeminent channel for segmented marketing, showed the impact. From 1980 to 1999, the volume of Standard A mail, the dominant class for direct mail marketing, grew from 29 percent to 43 percent of the total mail stream.[13] If one includes all the channels through which data-based marketing operates, the discipline captured 53 percent of all U.S. advertising spending in 2008.[14]

In summary, businesses' shift in the 1970s away from fixed and toward flexible arrangements of their productive resources enabled them to manufacture variety and occasioned a corresponding shift in the practice of marketing away from unitary content broadcast to all by mass media and toward variable content delivered to segments by media that can be addressed to households and individuals. The homogeneous consumer culture of the 1950s that expressed a commonly shared American Dream was displaced by the cultivation of difference among ever more narrowly defined groups—first, segments; then, niches; today, markets of one that make the ultimate promise, individuated self-expression. Data-based marketing, not just the direct mail industry but the whole way of looking at consumers—how we're defined, sized, assessed and addressed—was the leading edge of this shift, and it sets us up and brings us forth in its own particular way.

Notes

1 James Beniger, *The Control Revolution: Technological and Economic Origins of the Information Society* (Cambridge, MA: Harvard University Press, 1986) is comprehensive history of feedback systems in the U.S. economy up to the mid-20th century.

2 Those who saw a real break included John Kenneth Galbraith, *The New Industrial State* (New York: Houghton Mifflin, 1967); Alvin Toffler, *Future Shock* (New York: Random House, 1970); Daniel Bell, *The Coming of Post-Industrial Society: A Venture in Social Forecasting* (New York: Harper Colophon, 1973) and Peter F. Drucker, *Post-Capitalist Society* (New York: HarperCollins, 1993). Krishan Kumar, *Prophecy and Progress: The Sociology of Industrial and Post-Industrial Society* (New York: Penguin, 1978) and Frank Webster, *Theories of the Information Society* (London: Routledge, 2002) see it as a phase.

3 David Harvey, *The Condition of Post-Modernity: An Enquiry into the Origins of Cultural Change* (Oxford: Blackwell Publishing Ltd., 1990), 119—197 explains the shift from fixed to flexible arrangements. Other notable treatments include Manuel Castells, *The Information Age: Economy, Society and Culture: Volume 1—The Rise of Network Society* (Oxford: Blackwell, 1996); Michael Piore and Charles Sabel, *The Second Industrial Divide* (New York: Basic Books, 1984); Scott Lash

and John Urry, *The End of Organized Capitalism* (Cambridge, U.K.: Polity, 1987); Robert B. Reich, *The Work of Nations: Preparing Ourselves for 21ˢᵗ Century Capitalism* (New York: Vintage, 1991) and Lester Thurow, *The Future of Capitalism* (New York: Penguin Books, 1997).

4 Alexander R. Galloway, *Protocol: How Control Exists After Decentralization* (Cambridge, MA: The MIT Press, 2004), 158.

5 Roland Marchand, *Advertising the American Dream: Making Way for Modernity, 1920—1940* (Berkeley: University of California Press, 1985). Daniel Pope, *The Making of Modern Advertising* (New York: Basic Books, 1983) and Stuart Ewen, *Captains of Consciousness: Advertising and the Social Roots of Consumer Culture* (New York: McGraw-Hill, 1976) are also valuable histories.

6 The classic works are David Reisman with Nathan Glazer and Reuel Denny, *The Lonely Crowd: A Study of the Changing American Character* (New Haven: Yale University Press, 1950); William H. White Jr., *The Organization Man* (New York: Simon and Schuster, 1957); Vance Packard, *The Status Seekers* (New York: David McKay, 1959) and Erik Erikson, *Childhood and Society* (New York: W.W. Norton, 1950).

7 See Tom Frank, *The Conquest of Cool: Business Culture, Counterculture and the Rise of Hip Consumerism* (Chicago: University of Chicago Press, 1997).

8 Kevin G. Wilson, *Technologies of Control: The New Interactive Media for the Home* (Madison: University of Wisconsin Press, 1988), 35, quoted in Mark Poster, *The Mode of Information: Post-Structuralism and Social Context* (Chicago: University of Chicago Press, 1990), 75.

9 Occupational strata often appear prior to the technologies that propel their growth and crystallize their presence. For example, factory workers appeared when labor was divided up and rationalized, decades before power-driven mechanized factories appeared. According to Drucker, knowledge workers are neither the largest

nor the ruling group of our society but they are contemporary society's leading class and as such shape its character, leadership and
social profile.

10 Paul Starr and Ross Corson, "Who Will Have the Numbers? The
Rise of the Statistical Services Industry and the Politics of Public
Data" in William Alonso and Paul Starr, eds. *The Politics of Numbers*,
(New York: Russell Sage Foundation, 1987), 415—447 is a short
history of the consumer information business.

11 Dick Shaver, *The Next Step in Database Marketing: Consumer Guided
Marketing* (New York: John Wiley & Sons: 1996), 40.

12 John Goss, "Marketing the New Marketing: The Strategic Discourse of Geodemographic Information Systems," in John Pickles,
ed. *Ground Truth: The Social Implications of Geographic Information Systems* (New York: Guilford Press, 1995), 130—170. See also Jerry
L. Salvaggio, "Projecting a Positive Image of the Information Society" in Jennifer Daryl Slack and Fred Fejes, eds., *The Ideology of
the Information Age* (Norwood: Ablex Publishing Company, 1987),
146—157.

13 U.S. Census Bureau, *Statistical Abstract of the United States, 2000:*
Section 18: Communications and Information Technology, No.
936. "U.S. Postal Service—Summary: 1980 to 1999," www.census.
gov/prod/2001pubs/statab/sec18.pdf.

14 "Direct Marketing to Account for 53% of US Ad Spend in 2009,"
The Research Brief from the Center for Media Research Blog, December 5, 2008, www.mediapost.com/publications/?fa=Articles.
showArticle&art_aid=95711..

CHAPTER 3

THE DAYDREAMER AND
THE PROBABILITY

Dreams are but interludes, which fancy makes;
When monarch reason sleeps, this mimic wakes.
— John Dryden, "The Cock and the Fox" in *Fables*
(1697)

Like dreams, statistics are a form of wish fulfillment.
— Jean Baudrillard, *Cool Memories* (1987)

The word *communication* in everyday usage connotes transportation. An intended meaning is packaged into a message of words and images at Point A and then sent via some channel to Point B, where the message is unpacked and its meaning acquired. But this view understates the collaboration involved. The receiver at Point B must first pay attention to the message's arrival; unpack its contents; interpret its meaning, sometimes the way the sender intended, sometimes not and finally decide whether to apply the interpreted meaning to her own situation.

In Latin *com-* means *with,* and every communication is a collaboration, one that shapes the self-experience of the communicators. We all know this from everyday life. A conversation between parent and child, for example, or between doctor and patient—who says what to whom and how—reflects a set of assumptions about where each stands relative to the other and to the world that shapes who each can be within those conversations.

Public modes of address do this, too. All journalism, for example, even the sports pages, speaks to the citizen, someone who can weigh reported facts and attributed comments and come to his own conclusion. Marketing communications, which dominates public discourse in the consumer republic and to which all of us are incessantly exposed almost everywhere, addresses us in three ways. On a general level, all marketing communications tees us up as self-expressionists; its two disciplines, advertising and data-based marketing, conjure us up more narrowly as daydreamers and probabilities. The first two provide context and contrast, respectively, for understanding the third.

All marketing communications makes four assumptions about each of us. The first three are procedural: each of us has the right to desire, to choose and to buy the product. The fourth is substantive: each of us is centrally committed to lifestyle—the lifelong project of expressing one's self via particular assemblages of goods, services, practices, experiences, appearances and bodily dispositions. Critics from both the left and right have for ages scorned the commitment to lifestyle as vapid materialism and much worse. Much of their criticism is solid but typically critics on both sides omit self-expression's cultural history: it was born as critique and was as important as self-interest in the emergence of the modern self. Recalling this history helps explain what the critics haven't: why we enjoy experiencing ourselves as consumers and, more important here, why all marketing communications addresses us as self-expressionists.

In the Western canon, the precursor of our commitment to lifestyle can be found in Romanticism. This late 18th to- early 19th century cultural movement championed various forms of religio-aesthetic self-expression: sensibility, inner feelings and/or imagination. And it did so in part in protest, as a salutary alternative to the calculating rationality with which self-interest was pursued in the impersonal worlds of commerce and contracts.

Romanticism's chief British exponents, the poets Blake, Coleridge, Wordsworth, Keats and Shelley, were all critical of the then-emerging society for the primacy of utility as *the* source of value among men and for the primacy of the "cash nexus" as *the* social relation among them. Contemporary political conservatives such as Edmund Burke and Thomas Carlyle also rejected the idea of society as simply a neutral procedural arena defined by rules within which each individual is free to pursue his own advantage. As Carlyle explained, a society must be more than economic relationships:

> "Supply and demand" we will honor; and yet how many "demands" are there, entirely indispensable, which have to go elsewhere than to the shops, and produce quite other than cash, before they can get their supply.[1]

While they acknowledged the calculation of utility and the cash nexus, the conservatives found the glue of social life in the interrelation and continuity of human activities and the community's shared values in which they were rooted. The disintegrative effects of social atomism would in the next century become a theme of the Left as well, but 18th century liberalism championed individualism: *homo economicus* in economics, the Cartesian ego in philosophy, the novel hero in literature and the autonomy of consciousness, reason and perception everywhere else.

The poets sought even higher truths—God, Nature and Beauty—and found the path to those universals not in the shared life of the community but within the individual. Specifically, through the individual's imagination the spiritual nature of man was to be revealed, and the poets offered up their verses as private adventures to these transcendent glories. According to one scholar, Romanticism was a "prodigious effort to discover the world of spirit through the unaided efforts of the solitary soul."[2] These poets were not the first to claim that the artist revealed a higher kind of truth, but they were the first to claim autonomy for the individual artist in doing so and the individual's imagination as its source. In short, the Romantics legitimized self-expression and subjectivity.

A self-expressivist strain can be traced among our canonical philosophers, too; here's just the start and the finish. The pre-Romantic Jean-Jacques Rousseau is usually credited as the founder. His criticism of then-emerging society focused on what it had done to the individual; specifically, it had replaced the virtuous egoism of Rousseau's "natural man" (whom the Romantics renamed "noble savage") with an ignoble vanity that depended on others, on what *they* think of, expect from, admire in or despise in us. To regain our virtuous individualism we need to turn inward. Others before Rousseau had argued that one could trust one's inner feelings to *understand* the good. He took one radical step further. He argued that one's inner feelings could *define* the good; unity and wholeness were to be discovered within. The culmination of this strain among the philosophers is usually credited to the anti-Romantic Friedrich Nietzsche. For Nietzsche the world consisted of blind, chaotic and unspiritual forces for which there would never be resolution, compensation, reconciliation or any other way out. In an amoral universe, the only moral source that anyone could affirm lay beyond good and evil in the act of affirmation itself, in our ability to look into the maelstrom and say "yes" to everything. His *übermenschen* were those individuals who affirm life and overcome nihilism by way of self-creation, specifically self-differentiation. "We have art," he said, "that we may not perish from the truth."

Baudelaire, Balzac, Wilde and the Bloomsbury Group lived out aesthetic individualism in their personal lives, often brazenly and sometimes notoriously, but it was lesser minds who popularized it. *Fin-de*-siècle journalists, artists and bohemian hangers-on in Paris, London, New York and other capitals challenged the prevailing business-Christian ethic of industry, foresight and thrift and instead advocated living for the moment and the stylization of life. In short, they replaced salvation with self-realization.[3] Soon thereafter, the advertising industry co-opted the avant-garde position and turned it into a celebration of consumption as the path to self-expression.[4] The concept even got a slogan—"Life is an art."—from the 1923 best-seller *The Dance of Life* by pioneer sex researcher Havelock Ellis.

Two basic weaknesses in the credo were denounced right away and famously. According to Joseph Wood Krutch in *The Modern Temper* (1929), it promotes subjectivism. One can live life as an art, he argued, only if human life and history have no grand purpose, meaning or message, only if one abandons the notion that truths exist that owe their name to the fact that they correspond to something in the world outside, whether that something is revealed by religion or science. Instead, under the credo of life as art, the aims of self-expression, whether noble or neurotic, are private goals, not open to examination or critique.[5] It also promotes privatism, according to sociologist Robert S. Lynd. Already famous for *Middletown* (1929), his co-authored study of middle-class life in Muncie, Indiana, Lynd argued in the *President's Research Committee on Social Trends* (1933) that the credo was undermining *public* virtues, such neighborliness and social responsibility, and *social* sentiments, such as "all men are created equal" and "live and let live." Even worse, it fueled the growing belief that individual needs could be met at the shopping mall, that self-fulfillment could be purchased.[6]

The credo's strengths were and remain obvious. It certainly does liberate the individual. No longer controlled by conformity to community, whether villages and neighborhoods or tribes and religions, or by nature, whether by the seasons and terrain or by body types and age, we are free to be self-made. Living life as the art of self-expression, each of us can make herself up, albeit from raw materials provided by the marketplace. Like the artist, each of us has wide latitude in aims and methods with no judge or criteria other than to be true to her inner self. It also affirms the ultra-ordinary life of work and family that all modern politics—Marxist, liberal and conservative—define as the general welfare. In particular, it upholds the "householder ethos," the concerns of providing and caring for wife and children and the rich joys of family love as a web of relationships that give fullness and meaning to human life.[7] Indeed, a strong case has been made that in the affirmation of everyday life, individuals can and do connect to what philosophers call the "good."[8]

The strengths and weaknesses of our commitment to lifestyle have been argued at length many times before. Here, it suffices to recall that self-expression was as important as self-interest in the emergence of the modern self several centuries ago. In recent history, certainly from the 1920s onward, all marketing communications assumes that each of us is centrally committed to lifestyle as the means of our self-expressions, and every instance of such communication calls us up as self-expressionists. This assumption is the context within which advertising and data-based marketing conjure us up in their distinctive ways.

The Daydreamer

All advertising contains two implicit messages that some with good reason see as ideological. First, it's universally optimistic. For whatever problem advertising poses, it always presents a solution and does so with clarity and speed. Second, it's always progressive. Every instance asserts that given appropriate knowledge (about the product or service), we can "control the consequences of our deeds and shape our destinies."[9] Both promises are expressed in all advertising. More important here, the structure of the genre, its mode of address, in every instance calls us up as daydreamers.

That structure is drama: problem, solution and conclusion. A problem is posed: some peril of everyday life, like bad breath or lost credit cards, threatens the hero/heroine (warrior/maiden; good father/good mother). The solution appears: a *deus ex machina* in a wide variety of incredible guises—a wise confidant (hairdresser or manicurist), helpful factotum (genie or repairman), knowing expert (pharmacist or stock broker), super-human (athlete or entertainer), an allegorical figure (little man made of dough or a big man made of tires) and a menagerie of singing animals and dancing objects. The solution prompts the hero's/heroine's moment of insight, conversion or turning point, followed by the happy conclusion, usually peace of mind, self-esteem or a successful human relationship.[10]

Consumers do not expect rationality. To the contrary, advertising's mythic characters and their miraculous interventions are overt signals to the consumer that she can suspend her disbelief and put aside the critical faculties she would apply if the content were informational. But it's not. For the most part, advertising serves up nonreflective content to a passive audience in an associative frame of mind. Reverie, the interplay of listening and viewing with thinking and imagining, describes our half-conscious collaboration with advertising. Inhabiting the worlds we see and, just as easily, moving outside of them, mixing our external perceptions with our inner reflections, imaginary and real emotions, we take in what's out there and then create interior experiences that pleasure us.[11] In short, the consumer collaborates with advertising as a daydreamer.

Although daydreaming is as old as the hills, the cultural praise and legitimacy of our inner imaginings and the subjective experiential pleasure we take in them has also been traced to 18th Romanticism. Indeed, historical sociologist Colin Campbell proposes that a Romantic ethic of "autonomous imaginative hedonism" was as central to the spirit of consumerism as the Protestant ethic was to spirit of capitalism.[12]   Prior to the 18th century, Campbell argues, pleasure was sought through the senses: food, sex, music and laughter. Thus, elites had banquets, harems, musicians and clowns, while the masses had carnivals, their annual taste of the same. In contrast, the modern self replaced the sensory experience of the body with the emotional experience of the imagination—daydreams of finer lifestyles, novel goods, exotic experiences and so forth. According to Campbell, these images reflected a new "ability to create an illusion known to be false but felt to be true" and were created by the individual for self-consumption.

The evoking of interior pleasures was also a distinguishing feature of two cultural-economic developments of the 18th century, both of which were precursors to consumer culture: the rise of the novel-reading public and the emergence of the European fashion system.[13]   Art was seen the same way. Poet and essayist Joseph Addison was among many who argued that art pleases by evoking the action of the mind in apprehending color, sound and other sensations, that it's our interior response that pleases us and that both novelty and surprise, while having little value in themselves, were nevertheless often necessary to elicit this experience.[14] In other words, we learned as early as the 18th century how to pleasure ourselves with our imaginings.

Today, neuroscientists are trying to capture the physical expression of these imaginings. Using functional magnetic resonance imaging to scan the brain's reactions to different marketing actions, they found that we light up, particularly in the medial orbitofrontal cortex, in response to goods we expect to deliver more pleasant self-experiences.[15] In short, we get a cerebral shiver. "A little mist of energy ... rather like love but trivial" is how one mid-20th century cultural critic described it long before the neuroscientists arrived.[16] Of course, Average Joe doesn't need critics or scientists. He already knows all about this. The belief in subliminal advertising persists as urban legend because it captures our suspicion that something *is* going on just below consciousness that does stimulate us.[17]

Whether we are boobs being bamboozled by Madison Avenue, savvy consumers who greet commercial solicitations with ironic detachment, something in between or something else altogether is a different discussion. What's proposed here, with an aspiration to saying something as close to empirical as the phenomenon will allow, is that advertising as a mode of address conjures us up as daydreamers. That's how we collaborate with advertising's 30-second vignettes and storytelling snapshots; it wants our attention because it wants to trigger our associations. Perhaps, daydreaming as such, our subjective immersion into pleasurable self-contemplation, explains why we tolerate, even embrace, the genre. Maybe we don't want the marketer's steak at all; maybe it's our internal sizzles that we can't get enough of.

The Probability

Data-based marketing conjures us up in an entirely different way. The most basic difference is atomic. The daydreamer is carbon-based; she's human. The data-profile appears in silicon; it's an informational product. That is, with the data-profile we leave the physical world and cross the boundary into what Yale computer scientist David Gelernter calls the "mirror world"—the vast array of computer databases in which the details of our everyday lives (and much else besides) are stored, processed, exchanged and analyzed in order to inform others' decision making.

Just as individuals collaborate with advertising and co-create the daydreamer, we co-create the data profile by contributing the electronic traces that we leave behind whenever we use credit/debit cards, store/loyalty cards, mobile phones and toll plaza tags, whenever we request information, submit claims, register at Web sites, order tickets, donate to charities, return warranty cards, answer surveys or enter sweepstakes, supplemented by public records created by numerous government agencies.[18] These data fall into several large buckets:

- Personal data: Name, address, city, state, zip code, phone number, e-mail address

- Demographic data: Age, gender, marital status, presence of children, home value, education level
- Purchase data: What we bought, when and how much we spent
- Promotion data: The campaigns, offers and incentives to which we responded
- Consumer data: Category usage, brand preferences, purchase motivators and barriers
- Lifestyle data: Media usage, hobbies, interests, political affiliations, charitable donations and other psychograhic indicators[19]

Some consumer information brokers have more than 1,000 data points on each individual and household in their databases. In short, the digital detritus of our behaviors and choices in our everyday lives is the ectoplasm for our profiles in the datascape. From this data, marketers create profiles of us behind our backs after we've moved on.

Privacy defenders raise a hue and cry. What if Amazon were to sell to prospective employers lists of the books we bought? What if health insurers knew the illnesses that we looked up at WebMD? These and other alarms ring hollow because, for the most part, only tax agents and divorce lawyers want records about individuals or households. Everyone else wants groups. Records of individual- and household-level data do undergo a regular schedule of "data hygiene" procedures (monthly is typical among consumer information brokers) that help ensure completeness, accuracy, recency and other quality attributes. Those ministrations aside, however, the data just sit until someone queries the database, and all queries can be boiled down to one: how does this group differ from that group? In other words, applying a query to its database, the machine sorts individual records into group profiles,[20] turning data into information. In practice, queries generally are intended to inform decision making and be predictive, yielding this definition: data profiles are informational constructs of aggregated records that statistically differentiate the people associated with *these* records as more likely than the people associated with *those* records to conform to some end state desired by the analyst and on that basis justify and enable treating *these* persons differently from *those* persons.

Some profiles are simple. For example, a company can make a profile of its current customers and then target prospects who look like them; these look-alikes are better prospects. A little more sophisticated: a company can profile its best current customers and narrow its look-alike prospecting. Industry-specific versions are easy. A bank segments its current customers into those with relationship services (e.g., mortgages, investment accounts and CDs), those with transactional services (e.g., checking and savings accounts) and those with both types; it then profiles each segment and targets prospects who look like each.

Other groupings are more complex. For example, any company can and many do divide their customers into four groups based on how often the customer buys and how much the customer spends. The resulting four groups are customers who (1) buy often and spend a lot (best), (2) buy rarely but spend a lot (good), (3) buy often but spend little (good) and (4) buy rarely and spend little (worst). Some groupings are very complex, the result of analyses performed on hundreds of variables about each customer. A regression model, for example, calculates the correlation between each of a customer's many attributes and a dependent variable. The attribute with the strongest correlation with the dependent variable gets the highest weight in the model, the attribute with the next strongest correlation gets the next highest weight and so on. The result is a list of customer attributes rank ordered by the strength with which each attribute correlates with the dependent variable. Prospects whose rank-ordered attributes look like the rank-ordered attributes of existing customers are better.

Whether simple or complex, the purpose of all this slicing and dicing is the same: to predict which ones among us are more likely than others to buy, buy more often, pay full prices, respond to a promotion or behave in some other way that's profitable. That's why marketing solicitations that go directly to households and individuals focus on stimulating behavior, not reverie; the marketer's data analysis has already teed us up as statistically more likely than others to respond. So, those solicitations emphasize the immediate benefits of purchasing the product, carry a call to action, such as returning this post card or calling this number and stimulate that action with a discount, rebate or other limited-time incentive.

Dividing people into groups and treating them differently poses two issues. Although both affect individuals, they're social in structure and substance. First is the fairness in treating persons of one group differently from persons of another group. Second is the larger framework—here, the vision of the larger society—that defines which differences among us matter and how the resulting groups fit together. Transparency is a third issue, especially because the source of unfairness often resides in the rules applied to data, but it's procedural, not substantive.

Statistical differentiation as the basis for commercial discrimination has certain consequences that are logical and inescapable: cherry-picking at the high end, social dumping at the bottom and stereotyping everywhere in between.[21] When this commercial discrimination conflicts with other commitments and values, fairness issues arise. Following are two examples, both largely invisible. One discriminates against residents of Black neighborhoods, the other against loyal customers, regardless of race, color or creed.

A 2008 report by the Federal Reserve Bank of Boston found that credit card companies offer a higher credit line to residents of white neighborhoods than to *similarly qualified* residents of black neighborhoods. That neighborhood-level discrimination harms the black group and its individual members. A data rule compounds the harm to the individual. In determining an individual's credit score, the amount borrowed is compared with the amount available. The smaller this ratio, the higher one's credit score. All other things being equal, then, two borrowers with the same loan amount but different credit lines will get different credit scores. Black neighborhood residents are thus twice harmed, first by the lower credit lines available to them as members of a group and then by the lower credit scores as individuals that result when the individual's loan amount is weighted by the group's lower credit line.[22] Neither harm is readily visible, and the second resides in a rule.

The example that affects everyone, regardless of race, color or creed, is this: loyal customers are charged higher prices. This practice is unknown to most consumers but old news to marketers; loyal customers have always been charged more in part because they are willing to pay more. What's new is the spread of the data-driven solutions that enable discriminatory treatments of all types in the more thorough extraction of each customer's lifetime financial value. Thanks to customer relationship management (CRM) software, introduced in the mid-1990s, companies can now gather in one place all records relating to the same customer: products purchased, prices paid, purchase dates, promotion responses, service appointments, returns, complaints and payment history. This more complete data set enables companies to segment customers by profitability, the revenues they get from the customer minus the costs to acquire and keep her. On that basis, marketers spend more to acquire and keep those of us who are probably more profitable and less on those probably less so.[23] That's fair. But those profits we deliver include the prices we pay, and, profits notwithstanding, it still seems unfair to ask the more loyal to pay the higher prices.

Red-lining inside credit scoring, discriminatory pricing and other "fairness" issues abound because discrimination is the whole point of all this slicing and dicing. Of course, it cuts both ways; some get spiffed, others get stiffed. But every instance divides us in order to conquer us. It need not be these persons *rather than* those persons; it could be these persons *among* those persons, these persons *before* those persons, or these persons get *this* while those persons get *that*. Commercial discrimination takes many forms but, at bottom, is everywhere the same. Every targeted marketing campaign whether that targeting occurs through the mail, the Web, TV, cell phones, or even the cash register means that some marketer somewhere has compiled from one or more databases a temporary constellation of attributes about some of us in order to identify, address and target some smaller subgroup of us who, according to their data analyses, are more likely than others to buy once, buy more, buy again or provide some other business benefit.

The second social problem is more invidious because it's hard to see, even though it's in plain sight. Like perceiving the pattern of the tiles in a mosaic, it requires stepping back to see the vision of the larger society within which groups are defined and differentiated. These larger frameworks are the national segmentation schemas. The earliest were *Acorn* from CACI International for the United Kingdom and *PRIZM* from Claritas for the United States.[24]   Today, all the big brokers of consumer information, such as Experian, Acxiom and Harte Hanks, and media research companies, like MRI and Simmons, have proprietary schemas for the whole. So do many national brands and retailers; if not, they plug their in-house data into commercially available ones.

All work roughly alike: the record for each household and individual in their databases combines (at least) three sets of data. The first is geographic: area codes, zip codes, census tracts and their subunits. The second is demographic: age, marital status, educational level, income range and more. The third is psychographic: data on our values, attitudes and lifestyle interests. Geographic, demographic and psychographic data about households and individuals make us addressable, targetable and, marketers hope, persuadable.

Taking one giant step further, the national segmentation schemas do what their name implies: they segment the entire population into lifestyle-based clusters. Initially, we were parsed into neighborhood types, each with an appropriately descriptive label, such as Blue Blood Estates, Urban Gold Coast, Furs & Station Wagons, Pools & Patios, Blue-Collar Blues, Shotguns & Pickups, Coalburg & Corntown, Emerging Minorities and several dozen more. Now that commercial databases are rich with addressable individual- and household-level data, the neighborhoods are no longer necessary, and we can be targeted by lifestyle cluster wherever we happen to live. Within each cluster, homogeneity is assumed; even though it's not entirely true, it's true enough for most purposes. More important, like tiles in a mosaic, the clusters only make sense in the context of the whole.

In computer science such a whole is called an ontology. An ontology is a conceptualization of any particular activity, broken down into all the entities involved, their functions relative to the activity's goals and their relations with each other, so they can be represented within an information system. An ontology is then implemented on a computer so that the activities by the entities in the real world can be mirrored within the machine. Once an ontology has mapped out its view of an activity and implemented its map on a computer, actual entities and actual episodes of their activity are identified, verified, counted, compared, rearranged and evaluated in terms of the activity's goals. An ontology is not a given of nature; it's a construct.[25]

The ontology of the national segmentation schemas presents society as a socioeconomic stratification (SES) system. The primary hierarchal principle is class, specifically wealth, income and occupation, supplemented by the attributes that correlate with class: education and race. This core is then elaborated by applying additional attributes: geographic attributes that characterize different residential types and neighborhood environments, demographic attributes that differentiate households based on the kinship relations and the life stages of families within them and psychographic attributes, such as hobbies, interests, media habits and purchasing behaviors. In other words, the skeleton of these schemas is a vision of our SES system, with all its assumptions about what's important, how it works and how its parts relate, re-presented for marketers' purposes in commodity form as a mosaic of lifestyle-based clusters.

Unfortunately, the ontology of these national schemas is antiquated. The schemas do have more clusters today than originally, largely integrating demographic shifts, including delayed marriage, single parenthood, aging baby boomers, increasing longevity and immigration, but all see America's SES system largely as it emerged a century ago with the rise of the corporate form of industrial capitalism: old money, nouveau riches and power elites on top, professionals and upper management next, followed by white-, blue- and pink-collar wage earners, farm labor and migrant workers. This view is not wrong. This hierarchy and its groups are still with us. But there's not a hint that the SES system underneath the lifestyle schemas may have or may be changing in any fundamental ways.

Real life suggests otherwise. It is universally acknowledged that the growing importance of information-based goods and services has already led us into a post-industrial economy, that the rapidly growing strata of knowledge workers is altering society's occupational structure and that all work is being transformed into provisional labor. These changes are in progress, and many questions about them—whether the post-industrial economy is a real break or just a phase of capitalism's history, whether knowledge workers are a leading strata or the 21st century's proletariat—are far from settled. It's certainly not the job of marketers or their tools to wrestle with changes in our SES system. At the same time, these changes are huge and they've been operating at full tilt and in plain sight for over four decades. Everyone has experienced some impact from at least one, and they all condition our considerations and decisions as consumers and in other capacities. In other words, the schemas aren't wrong; they still work. They just don't speak to much of what we're actually experiencing in and what's distinctive to our times.

Making matters worse, the schemas are self-perpetuating for three good reasons. First, researchers don't like to change their yardsticks because it compromises the ability to make comparisons over time. So there's a professional preference for keeping things the same. Second, all data-based representation schemas are limited by their ontologies. A system for tracking an object's location, for example, will not be affected by and will not measure changes in its color. So, too, the national segmentation schemas cannot accept inputs that don't already fit into their conceptual maps. Finally, feedback loops or cybernetic systems are circular. By definition, feedback is a method for controlling a system by reinserting into it the results of its past performance. In the decision-making regime of data-based marketing, decision makers see and make decisions about the world through the lens of a specific data model. We consumers then interact with the world that those decisions shaped, generating more data within that model, informing the next round of decisions *ad indefinitum*.[26] In short, the yardstick is stable, the ontology closed and the feedback circular—all quite legitimate reasons for the schemas to be self-perpetuating.

Using information systems to integrate consumers and producers is, to critics, an invidious form of social control; to champions, it's an advanced form of functional optimization. Both are a bit abstract. The schemas examined here assume and act within a more specific context. They conceive and subsume all of us under and within a view of society as a socioeconomic stratification system and a particular one that makes assumptions about what's important in this society, how it works and how its parts relate to each other and to the whole. In other words the clusters are the tiles while the schemas are the pattern in the mosaic.

While the social problem of fairness derives from dividing and then treating us differently, the social problem here derives from unifying us all under a particular vision of our society and then making that vision both real and self-perpetuating through the follow-on decisions made about the face of the world, the physical and symbolic terrains of our lived experience. As explained earlier, these decisions start but do not end with the individual. It's not just who gets what offers, such as the interest rate on a home mortgage or an auto loan, the rewards on a credit card, the terms of a mobile calling plan or the premium on an insurance policy. Beyond individuals, these schemas determine what stores open up in the mall, the goods they stock and the prices they charge, the channels available from the cable service, the movies booked for neighborhood theaters and more. They determine which high schools the U.S. Army targets for recruiting, which medical specialties are offered at local hospitals, which neighborhoods are rezoned for development and so on.

Moreover, while these and all other decisions are made independently, they are not discrete from each other. Rather, they are layered, tangled and textured into an ecology of representation and action that continually monitors, adjusts and readjusts the made environment toward or away from statistical patterns of consumer behaviors. In short, ersatz versions of us go into databases, ersatz answers about us come out and we must all live with the consequences of all the decisions made on that basis. This is how data-based marketing shapes the built environment as readymade for our consumption. [27]

The data profile is the corresponding shape that humans take inside the machine as readymade to consume the built environment. This does not violate the individual's privacy or anything else. Rather, the individual is reconstituted inside this decision-making regime as a probability, an informational entity with properties of its own.

Our assimilation into the machine begins, of course, in the carbon-based world. Our choices and behaviors in everyday life, captured continuously, are the lifeblood of this whole apparatus. Thus, our carbon-based selves and silicon representations change in tandem but, although they are based on us, they are not us. As explained in the recounting of the birth of social statistics, whenever human affairs are apprehended through the lens of numbers, individuals and our qualities disappear because data cannot capture the sources of individuality. Instead, the lens must focus on observable, common and variable attributes. It documents our individual states on those attributes in order to sort us by how we vary on those attributes. In short, the individual is reduced to an ersatz person, stripped of what data cannot measure about individuals and described by variable attributes that are useful to commerce and administration.

Upon leaving the carbon-based world, the data are placed inside the records of databases. Although regularly refreshed, the data just sit in the record as raw material, a resource waiting in reserve and on call to help others fulfill their purposes. In other words, before any statistical procedure is applied, the behaviors and choices of our everyday lives have been collected and repurposed into means for others' ends.

The data profile is born when some "other" actually queries the database. The machine answers a query by applying a statistical procedure that sorts records into profiles, turning data into information. The profile doesn't exist until called up. As an informational entity, it is contingent; it depends on the other for its existence.

The profile depends on the querier for its substance, too, because the profile in every instance is relative to the observer. Obviously, the profile is partial; not all of our attributes are relevant to every query. The converse is more important. The attributes that *are* included—those identified by the statistical procedure as most relevant to the query—make each profile specific to the observer. Some social critics complain of a "self multiplied by databases" not because every one of us is conjured up into profiles thousands, perhaps tens of thousands, of times daily (which we are), but because we are never the same person twice; indeed, we're never our own person even once. The profile's particulars are always specific to the query, and the profile as a whole is always specific to the eye of the beholder.

Finally, the profile is probabilistic. Designed to inform decision making, statistical procedures are applied in order to conjure up some us as more likely than others to conform to the end state desired by the observer. French philosopher Jean Baudrillard called statistics a form of wish fulfillment because every profile portrays us as the observer's desire.

In general, as long as numbers define humans in a common language, we can be submitted to assembly, disassembly, investment and exchange. The data profile is a version of this transformation. Based on the data of our everyday lives, it's part human, part machine—contingent, relative, and probabilistic. In short, the subject has been reconstituted as a manipulatable element of the object and the human assimilated into the machine.

Individuals are largely passive in the creation and use of data profiles. (The few steps we can take are reviewed in Appendix I.) Our lack of involvement is unfortunate given the importance of their use in the decisions that others make about us and our world. At the same time, this is certainly an achievement. Modern life would be impossible if we had not gone about slicing and dicing up both humans and nature. The peril occurs if this way of apprehending human affairs becomes predominant. As explained in the recounting of the crisis of capitalism in the 1970s and the triumph of data-based marketing over the three decades since, that's exactly what's happened. Going forward, however, we face a different situation: the opportunity to build, manage and promote our own cyberpersonas. They aren't created on a clean sheet of paper, of course; the tools available to us shape how we can present ourselves in cyberspace. But that's also the point. Tools are available today with new ones coming tomorrow, and like much else in cyberspace, they put power in the hands of users.

Notes

1 Quoted in Raymond Williams, *Culture and Society, 1780—1950* (New York: Harper & Row, 1966), 83.

2 C.M. Bowra, *The Romantic Imagination* (Oxford: Oxford University Press, 1969), 23.

3 T.J. Jackson Lears, "From Salvation to Self-Realization: Advertising and the Therapeutic Roots of Consumer Culture, 1880—1930," in T.J. Jackson Lears and Richard Wrightman Fox, eds., *The Culture of Consumption: Critical Essays in American History* (New York: Pantheon, 1983).

4 Pierre Bourdieu, *Distinction: A Social Critique of the Judgment of Taste* (Cambridge, MA: Harvard University Press, 1984), 318—371 argues that the project of making an art of life reflects the particular social position of workers at ad agencies who universalized their own attraction to the superficial aristocratic qualities of style and refinement as a way to establish social distinction. Thorstein Veblen, *The Theory of the Leisure Class* (1899) had already critiqued the "conspicuous consumption" of the *nouveau riches;* the democratization of "life as art" among middle-class Americans was a later and different development.

5 For recent critiques along this line, see Zygmunt Bauman, *Freedom* (Minneapolis: University of Minnesota Press, 1988), esp. chapter 3 and Michael Featherstone, "Lifestyle and Consumer Culture," *Theory, Culture and Society,* vol. 4 (1987), 55—70.

6 See Robert S. Lynd and A. C. Hanson, "The People as Consumers," in *President's Research Committee on Social Trends: Recent Social Trends in the United States* (New York: McGraw-Hill, 1933), 857—911.

7 It's worth noting that in contemporary America a disproportion-ate share of retail sales are gifts, including greeting cards, toiletries, cosmetics, stationary, books and art. See Michael Schudson, *Advertising, the Uneasy Persuasion: Its Dubious Impact on American Society* (New York: Basic Books, 1984), 135—143. .

8 Charles Taylor, *Sources of the Self: The Making of Modern Identity* (Cambridge, MA: Harvard University Press, 1989) offers this phil-osophical assessment. More narrowly, Albert O. Hirschman, *The Passions and the Interests: Political Arguments for Capitalism before Its Triumph* (Princeton: Princeton University Press, 1977) explains how in the 17th and 18th centuries the pursuit of material interests, previously denounced as avarice, was recast as *le doux commerce* and assigned the role of containing the unruly, dangerous and destruc-tive pursuits of glory and domination that had bred wars and aris-tocratic display.

9 Walter Cummins, "Love and Liquor: Modernism and Postmod-ernism in Advertising and Fiction in Mary Cross, ed., *Advertising and Culture: Theoretical Perspectives* (Westport: Praeger, 1996), 62. See also Schudson, 215.

10 Martin Esslin, "Aristotle and the Advertisers: The Television Commercial Considered as a Form of Drama" in Horace Newcomb, ed., *Television: The Critical View* (New York: Oxford University Press, 1987), 304—318. Legendary copywriter Howard Luck Gossage ex-plored the magical dimension of advertising in "That Old Black, White, or Pango Peach Magic," *Harper's Magazine* (March 1961).

11 On reverie, see Ron Burnett, *How Images Think* (Cambridge, MA: The MIT Press, 2004), esp. 40—56. In an earlier age this same phenomenon was understood as "low involvement learning"; see Herbert E. Krugman, "The Impact of Television Advertising: Learning without Involvement," *Public Opinion Quarterly* 29 (1965), 349—356.

12 Colin Campbell, *The Romantic Ethic and the Spirit of Modern Consumerism* (Cambridge, MA: Blackwell, 1987)

13 Anne Hollander, *Seeing through Clothes* (New York: Viking, 1978), 362. On novels and the imaginary, see Mark Poster, *What's the Matter with the Internet* (Minneapolis: University of Minnesota Press, 2001), 82—86.

14 Walter Jackson Bate, *From Classic to Romantic: Premises of Taste in Eighteenth Century England* (New York: Harper & Row, 1961), 98—99.

15 Hilke Plassmann, John O'Doherty, Baba Shiv and Antonio Rangel, "Marketing Actions Can Modulate Neural Representations of Experienced Pleasantness," *Proceedings of the National Academy of Science,* vol. 105 (January 22, 2008), 1050—1054 and Martin Lindstrom, *Buyology: Truth and Lies about Why We Buy* (New York: Doubleday, 2008).

16 George W. S. Trow, *Within the Context of No Context* (New York: Atlantic Monthly Press, 1997), 46—47. See also James B. Twitchell, *Adcult USA* (New York: Columbia University Press, 1996), 52.

17 See Leslie Savan, *The Sponsored Life: Ads, TV, and American Culture* (Philadelphia: Temple University Press, 1994), 61—64 on the popular belief in subliminal advertising.

18 In practice, public and private data interpenetrate; see Howard Radest, "The Public and the Private: An American Fairy Tale," *Ethics,* vol. 89 (April 1979), 280—291.

19 One data set is omitted from the text but discussed in Appendix I: one's social security number, bank account number, driver's license number or military ID number. They are called *personally identifying information* because they are used to authenticate individuals and thereby enable access to resources, including financial accounts.

20 The word *profile* is used here metaphorically, embracing all profiles, clusters, segmentations, correlated factors, algorithms and other data models used by marketing statisticians and data-based marketers to represent human beings by categorization and classification, especially those who seek to predict future needs and wants based on aggregated past choices and behaviors.

21 See Oscar H. Gandy, Jr., "It's Discrimination, Stupid!" in J. Brook and I. Boal, eds., *Resisting the Virtual Life. The Culture and Politics of Information* (San Francisco: City Lights Books, 1995), 35—47. The only thing worse than bias is invisibility, and it is well known that certain population segments—most notably, African Americans, Hispanic Americans, rural residents, the poor and immigrants—leave fewer electronic traces and as a result are less likely to appear in the datascape and the segmentation schemes derived from it. Because these population segments are rarely attractive to marketers, this issue rarely surfaces.

22 Ethan Cohen-Cole, "Credit Card Redlining," Working Paper No. QAU08-1, Federal Reserve Bank of Boston, February 26, 2008.

23 Among the myriad of books on CRM solutions, Ronald S. Swift, *Accelerating Customer Relationships: Using CRM and Relationship Technologies* (Upper Saddle River: Prentice Hall: 2001) provides a good overview. For a critical perspective, see "The Wealth and Poverty of Networks: Tackling Social Exclusion," *Demos Collection,* Issue 12 (1997).

24 Paul A Longley and Graham Clarke, eds., *GIS for Business and Service Planning,* (New York: John Wiley & Sons, 1995) and Michael Weiss, *The Clustering of America* (New York: Harper & Row, 1988) are descriptive accounts of these systems in the United Kingdom and United States, respectively.

25 Philip E. Agre, "Surveillance and Capture: Two Models of Privacy," *Information Society,* 10 (April – June, 1994), 101—127.

26 See Terry Curtis, "The Information Society: A Computer-Generated Caste System" and Oscar H. Gandy Jr., "The Political Economy of Communications Competence" in Vincent Mosco and Janet Wasko, eds., *The Political Economy of Information* (Madison: University of Wisconsin Press, 1988), 95—107 and 108—124, respectively, and the earlier works that both cite.

27 Geographers and urban planners have been particularly concerned with the impacts on our physical space; see Stephen Graham, "Spaces of Surveillent-Simulation: New Technologies, Digital Representations and Material Geographies," *Environment and Planning: Society and Space,* vol. 16, (1998), 483—504 and John Pickles, ed., *Ground Truth: The Social Implications of Geographic Information Systems* (New York: Guilford Press, 1995).

INTERLUDE: SATIRICAL STATISTICS

There are three kinds of lies:
lies, damned lies and statistics.

> —Benjamin Disraeli, attributed by Mark Twain,
> "Chapters of My Autobiography" (1907)

In developing this book, I came across a few satires of statistics that relate to the themes addressed here. They need only the briefest introductions.

The first is the oldest, an excerpt from Honoré de Balzac's *Physiology of Marriage* (1829). The second chapter on "Conjugal Statistics" attempts to quantify the number of women who qualify as marriageable, and the parody is riddled with assumptions masquerading as facts and descriptions turned into evaluations.

The best known is W. H. Auden's "The Unknown Citizen." This often-anthologized 1940 poem explores the root-level limitation of data, that it cannot count what counts most to humans. Specifically, although Auden's Bureau of Statistics rattles off a long list of diverse data points about his everyman, it cannot say at the end of the day whether he's free or happy and, worse, the Bureau doesn't know that it doesn't know.

Stanislaw Lem offers an even broader critique. His book review of *One Human Minute,* a fictitious compendium of everything that happens on Earth in 60 seconds, e.g., the tonnage of breast milk suckled, sperm ejaculated, poop

pooped and so on, explores how statistics shapes our percep-
tual boundaries in several ways. Most important, he argues
that statistical aggregates obscure individual experience but
concludes that his argument, lacking statistics to back it up,
remains a generality.

Russian émigré artists Vitaly Komar and Alexander
Melamid illustrate how quantitative methods cannot be applied to qualitative matters. With the help of The Nation
Institute, they surveyed consumers in 10 countries about what
they want in an oil painting and then produced paintings
that conformed to each nation's survey findings. The paintings can be found online at http://awp.diaart.org/km. The
interview except focuses on the poll as democratic truth.

Natalie Jeremijenko doesn't bother with the human
meanings of numbers. She aimed motion-detecting video
cameras at San Francisco's Golden Gate Bridge to capture
jumpers in the act. Although unanticipated seagull inter-
ference caused excessive triggering, her glowing cost-benefit
analysis explains how applying the logic of information to
suicide not only measures but actually generates economic
value   The question of why is not in her frame.

HONORÉ DE BALZAC, "CONJUGAL STATISTICS"

The government has been occupied for some twenty years in discovering how many acres of wood, of grass, of vines and of fallow are contained in the realm of France; it has even gone farther and calculated the number of each species of animals. Nor have our officials stopped there, they have counted the perches of wood, the pounds of beef, the quarts of wine, the number of apples and of eggs consumed annually in Paris. But no one has concerned himself, either for the honor of marriage, or in the interests of people getting married, or for the advance of morality and the perfecting of human institutions, to take a census of respectable women. What! Can a French minister answer any question as to the number of men he has under arms, the number of spies, the number of employees, the number of scholars, but as to virtuous wives—nothing? If the fancy took a king of France to seek his august consort among his subjects, the government could not even lead him to the flock of most white sheep from which to make his choice!

Let us make up for the negligence of the government by attempting for ourselves a classification and enumeration of the female sex in France. In this we claim the attention of all friends of public morals and appoint them judges of our procedure. We shall try to be liberal enough in our estimates and exact enough in our deductions to gain a general acceptance for the results of our analysis.

The evidence from which we start is the discovery of statisticians, that in France the poor number eighteen millions, the independent ten millions, and the rich two millions. There exist therefore in France only six million women with whom men of taste concern themselves ... Let us subject these social elect to a philosophic scrutiny.

We can safely assert that the husbands of twenty years standing are over the danger of amorous invasion and have no longer to fear the scandal of the divorce-court. And so from our six millions we subtract some two million adorable women, who being past forty have seen all they desire of the world ... Beautiful they may still be but ... they have to find other interests to make life supportable; they throw themselves into religion, or else into cats and dogs, manias that are as harmless as God.

The estimates of population published by the Office of Longitude authorize us to subtract from the remainder another two millions, these being the number of little girls;' pretty enough to make the mouth water, they still have to learn the A.B.C. of life ...

Now of the two million left any reasonable man will allow us to write off a hundred thousand, as unhappily born ugly, hunch-backed, crazy, rickety, sickly, blind or mutilated ... [T]hey must remain spinsters always, and so will have no opportunity to offend against the sacred laws of marriage.

And it will be granted surely, that another hundred thousand become Sisters of Saint Camilla, Sisters of Charity, nuns of all sorts, teachers, lady-companions, etc.

Lastly ... we must eliminate another half million units, as daughters of Baal who only give pleasure to the unrefined. Under this head we include, without fear that they will suffer by association, all: kept women, dress-makers, shop-girls, drapers, actresses, singers and dancers, governesses, chamber-maids, etc. ... Their code, justly condemned by a fastidious society, has the advantage of not binding them to their men, morally or legally. As these women break no public vows, they are no concern of a work devoted exclusively to legitimate marriages.

It is easy to prove the justice of our analysis, one test alone will suffice. A woman's life divides itself into three distinct periods, the first being from the cradle to the marriage-bed, the second being the years of marriage, the third and last beginning at that critical age when nature brutally serves a writ of eviction on the passions. These three stages of life, being roughly equal in duration, should divide in equal numbers a given quantity of women. Thus in a mass of six millions there should be found, neglecting the fractions which may be left to the learned to work out, about two million girls between the ages of one and eighteen, two million women of eighteen at least and forty at most, and two million old women. Further, the caprices of the social state have sub-divided the two million marriageable women into three unequal classes, as follows: those who for any of the reasons above given remain spinsters, those whose husbands care little as to their virtue, and finally the million legitimate women who are to be the subject of our study.

You see now from this careful count of the female population, that there hardly exists in France a little flock of a million white sheep; and into that favored fold all the wolves are trying to find an entrance. But this million of women, already sifted on the table, must now be passed through a fine sieve.

To calculate more exactly the degree of confidence which a man should have in his wife, let us suppose for a moment that all wives are going to deceive their husbands. This hypothesis still allows us to subtract a twentieth, as the proportion of young people married but yesterday, who will be true to their vows at least for a period. Another twentieth at least will be ill; this is surely not to magnify the pains that beset humanity. Certain conditions of the man, said to destroy his empire over the heart of woman, as ugliness or melancholy or fatness, will claim another twentieth.

Again, adultery does not establish itself in the heart of woman instantly like a pistol-shot. ... [T]here is always a struggle [and] it would be an insult to the modesty of France ... to represent the duration of this struggle by no more than a twentieth of all wives ... [W]e have to take into account that certain of the sick wives will keep their lovers even amid the medicine-bottles ... these will balance a number of those still fighting for their virtue and will acquit us of underestimating the force of modesty. Out of regard for the same ... we shall estimate it at a fortieth.

These subtractions reduce our total to little more than eight hundred thousand wives, when, it is a question of determining how many will commit a breach of conjugal faith. Before going farther let us ask, who would not like to believe that these women are all virtuous? Are they not the flower of the land? Are they not all in the spring of life, radiant with youth and beauty, with life and love? To believe in their virtue is a kind of social religion, for they are the ornament of the world and the glory of France. In the bosom of this million we must discover

THE NUMBER OF VIRTUOUS WOMEN

THE NUMBER OF RESPECTABLE WOMEN.

This investigation and the distinguishing of these two categories require two entire Meditations which shall 'serve as appendix to this one.[1]

W.H. AUDEN, "THE UNKNOWN CITIZEN"

He was found by the Bureau of Statistics to be
One against whom there was no official complaint,
And all the reports on his conduct agree
That, in the modern sense of an old-fashioned word, he was
a saint,
For in everything he did he served the Greater Community.
Except for the War till the day he retired
He worked in a factory and never got fired,
But satisfied his employers, Fudge Motors Inc.
Yet he wasn't a scab or odd in his views,
For his Union reports that he paid his dues,
(Our report on his Union shows it was sound)
And our Social Psychology workers found
That he was popular with his mates and liked a drink.
The Press are convinced that he bought a paper every day
And that his reactions to advertisements were normal in ev-
ery way.
Policies taken out in his name prove that he was fully in-
sured,
And his Health-card shows he was once in hospital but left it
cured.
Both Producers Research and High-Grade Living declare
He was fully sensible to the advantages of the Installment
Plan
And had everything necessary to the Modern Man,
A phonograph, a radio, a car and a frigidaire.
Our researchers into Public Opinion are content
That he held the proper opinions for the time of year;
When there was peace, he was for peace: when there was war,
he went.
He was married and added five children to the population,

Which our Eugenist says was the right number for a parent of his generation.

And our teachers report that he never interfered with their education.

Was he free? Was he happy? The question is absurd:

Had anything been wrong, we should certainly have heard.[2]

STANISLAW LEM, "ONE HUMAN MINUTE"

ONE HUMAN MINUTE
J. Johnson and S. Johnson
Moon Publishers
London—*Mare Imbrium*—New York, 1988

This book presents what all the people in the world are doing, at the same time, in the course of one minute ... The writing of such a book—an honest, uncontrived book about everything at once, a book that would overshadow all others—seemed a total impossibility. Even I could not imagine the sort of book it would be ...

So, the task the authors of *One Human Minute* set themselves did not look plausible. In effect, were I to tell someone who has not yet seen the book that it contains few words, that it is filled with tables of statistics and columns of numbers, he would look upon the undertaking as a flop, even as insanity. Because what can be done with hundreds of pages of statistics? ...

Consequently, the idea—to show sixty seconds in the lives of all the human beings who coexist with me—had to be worked out as if it were a plan for a major campaign. The original concept, though important, was not enough to ensure success. The best strategist is not the one who knows he must take the enemy by surprise, but the one who knows how to do it ...

[T]he statistics of Chapter One are beyond reproach. They tell how many people there are—and thus how many living bodies—in each minute of the 525,600 minutes of the year. How many bodies means the amount of muscle, bone, bile, blood, saliva, cerebrospinal fluid, excrement, and so one. Naturally, when the thing to be visualized is of a very great order of magnitude, a popularizer readily resorts to comparative imagery. The Johnsons do the same. So, were all humanity taken together in one place, it would occupy three hundred billion liters, or a little less than a third of a cubic kilometer. It sounds like a lot. Yet the world's oceans hold 1,285 million cubic kilometers of water, so if all human-ity—those five billion bodies—were cast into the ocean, the water level would rise less than a hundredth of a millimeter. A single splash, and Earth would be forever unpopulated.

After this, under an epigraph from T. S. Eliot saying that existence is "birth, and copulation, and death," come new fig-ures. Every minute, 34.2 million men and women copulate. Only 5.7 percent of all intercourse results in fertilization, but the combined ejaculate, at a volume of forty-five thousand liters a minute, contains 1,990 billion (with deviations in the last decimal place) living spermatozoa. The same number of female eggs could be fertilized sixty times an hour with a minimal ratio of one spermatozoon to one egg, in which im-possible case three million children would be conceived per second. But this, too, is only a statistical manipulation.

Pornography and our modern life style have accustomed us to the forms of sexual life. You would think that there was nothing left to reveal, nothing to show that would shock. But, presented in statistics, it comes as a surprise. Never mind—the game of comparisons which is put to use again: for in-stance, the stream of sperm, forty-three tons of it, discharged into vaginas per minute—its 430,000 hectoliters is compared with the 37,850 hectoliters of boiling water produced at each eruption of the largest geyser in the world (at Yellowstone). The geyser of sperm is 11.3 times more abundant and shoots without intermission. The image is not obscene. A person can be aroused sexually only within a certain range of mag-nitudes. Acts of copulation, when shown in great reduction or great enlargement, do not elicit any sexual response. Arousal, an inborn reaction, occurs as a reflex in certain cen-ters in the brain, and does not manifest itself in conditions that exceed visual norms. Sexual acts seen in reduced dimen-sions leave us cold, for they show creatures the size of ants. Magnification, on the other hand, arouses disgust, because the smoothest skin of the most beautiful woman will then look like a porous, pale surface from which protrude hairs as thick as fangs, while a sticky, glistening grease oozes from the ducts of the sebaceous glands.

The surprise I spoke of has a different cause. Humanity pumps 53.4 billion liters of blood per minute, but that red river is not surprising; it must flow to sustain life. At the same time, humanity's male organs eject forty-three tons of semen, and the point is that though each ejaculation is also an ordinary physiological act, for the individual it is irregular, intimate, not overly frequent, and even not necessary. Besides, there are millions of old people, children, voluntary and involuntary celibates, sick people, and so forth. And yet that white stream flows with the same constancy as the red river system. The irregularity disappears when the statistics take in the whole Earth, and that is what surprises. People sit down to tables set for dinner, look for refuse in garbage dumps, pray in chapels, mosques, and churches, fly in planes, ride in cars, sit in submarines carrying nuclear missiles, debate in parliaments; billions sleep, funeral processions walk through cemeteries, bombs explode, doctors bend over operating tables, thousands of college professors simultaneously enter their classrooms, theater curtains lift and drop, floods swallow fields and houses, wars are waged, bulldozers on battlefields push uniformed corpses into ditches; it thunders and lightnings, it is night, day, dawn, twilight; but no matter what happens that forty-three-ton impregnating stream of sperm flows without stop, and the law of large numbers guarantees that it will be as constant as the sum of solar energy striking Earth. There is something mechanical about this, inexorable, and animallike. How can one come to terms with an image of humanity copulating relentlessly through all the cataclysms that befall it, or that it has brought upon itself …

Again we have the dilemma on which the first critics of this book broke their teeth. Is the terrible predominance of evil over good, of malice over loving kindness, of stupidity over intelligence, the true balance sheet of the human

world? Or is it the result, in part, of the computers and the
statistical viewpoint?

It is easier to give the tonnage per minute that the sex
industry produces—the mountains of genital appliances,
photographs, special clothing, chains, whips, and other accessories that facilitate the application of our reproductive
physiology to perverted practices—than to measure, weigh,
or *simply observe* human love in its nontechnological manifestations. Surely, when people love one another—and it is
hard to doubt that there are hundreds of millions who do—
when they remain faithful to their erotic or parental feelings,
there is no measure, no apparatus, that can record *that* and
grind it in the statistical mill. With sadomasochism, on the
other hand, with rape, murder, or any perversion, there are
no such difficulties: statistical theory is at our service.

The industrialization of emotion in all its aspects—say
the indignant critics of *One Human Minute*—is an utter impossibility. There cannot be, nor ever will be, devices, har-
nesses, salves, aphrodisiacs, or any sort of "meters" to abet or
measure filial or maternal love; no thermometers to gauge
the heat of lovers' passions. That their temperature is sometimes fatally high, we learn only indirectly from the statistics
on suicides resulting from unrequited love. Such love is out
of fashion in the modern world, and any writer who devotes
his works to love alone will not make it into the literary Par-
nassus.

There is no denying the merit of such arguments as
these; the trouble is that without the backing of facts and
figures they remain generalities.[3]

NATALIE JEREMIJENKO, BUREAU OF INVERSE TECHNOLOGY, SUICIDE BOX [SBX]

The **bit Suicide Box** is a motion detection video system designed to capture vertical activity. Unit includes BIT camera, motion capture card, analysis software and utility concealment casing. In standard operation any vertical motion in frame will trigger the camera to record to disk.

Bureau installed the Suicide Box for trial application in range of the Golden Gate Bridge California 1996; an initial deployment period [100 days] metered 17 bridge events. System efficacy: Suicide Box system supplied public, frame-accurate data of a social phenomenon not previously accurately quantified …

ENGINEER'S REPORT, SUiCIDE BOX [SBX.3] Filed Jan 23. 1997

… The 100 test days of the second deployment period captured 17 events, averaging a rate 0.17suicides/day. This compares to the 0.13 rate calculated using Port Authority data averaged over the last two years. Assuming that the weather has neither positive nor negative effect on likelihood of jumping; that in San Francisco conditions of poor visibility can be more than 60% of total time; and that likelihood of jumping is equal from all parts of the bridge; this brings the suicide rate closer to 0.68 suicides/day and suggests that the estimated rate of this phenomenon in the previous accounts is too small by a factor of 4.

Using this projected figure and a mid-range value of life estimate (that is, the National Highway and Transport Safety Authority figure used in the cost-benefit analysis of the 55 mile per hour limit legislation of $500,000 dollars per life) we can recalibrate the rate of loss in economic terms as $182—$238 per day. This is less than 1% of the revenue generated at the tollgates.

... While there are other databases that provide correlates to the suicide rates ... there is none known that has the capacity to store video images of their source statistical data ... The Bureau has not only produced a method for the consistent collection of video enhanced comprehensive data ... but has done pioneering work to index this data to market indicators ...

The first application of this data is the opportunity to characterize the value of suicide. Legislators ... are currently divided between the 'willingness to pay' and the 'human capital' (or foregone earnings) approaches. The willingness-to-pay measure is derived from estimates of how much individuals are willing to pay to reduce their probability of death by small amounts, while the 'human capital' measure is based on estimates of the present value of foregone earnings due to premature death.

Using the BIT SUICIDE BOX data, a robust and market responsive value of life can be calculated, using essentially an inverse correspondence of the value of suicide. The rate of suicide can be taken to represent the general 'willingness-to-die' as an averaged phenomenon. This value, quantified by the amount of money spent on the prevention measures ... provides a base line measure for the inverse of the value of life. An important baseline adjustment, this data captures the value of life at the rare moment when the choice is reduced to its uncomplicated binary decision.

The value of suicide has previously been extremely hard to quantify and represent. It has unlike many other aspects of health care, life, death etc., resisted commodification. That is, it is not subject to a service sector, package tours, instructional kits or market predictability. The failure to commodify suicide and its images and enter it into the systems of exchange and value has meant that it has been undervalued, worse, has not had an explicit value at all. The work of the SUICIDE BOX, in its imaging of suicide, recovers this statistical representation as visual rendering, and quantifies what it is to render suicide in the logic of information.[4]

JOANN WYPIJEWSKI, ED.,
PAINTING BY THE NUMBERS:
KOMAR AND MELAMID'S
SCIENTIFIC GUIDE TO ART

Beginning on December 10, 1993, trained professionals working from a central, monitored location in Indiana telephoned Americans to find out what they want in art—fine art, specifically painting. For eleven days the survey continued, as people throughout the forty-eight contiguous states pondered: soft curves or sharp angles? Brush strokes or smooth surfaces? "Realistic looking" or "different-looking … On and on, for an average of twenty-four minutes, until all 102 questions had been asked. When it was over, 1,001 adult Americans had been interviewed. They were a statistically representative group, having been selected from all households by a random-probability sampling procedure that included unlisted numbers and was stratified according to state. Their collective responses, the poll results, are statistically accurate within a margin of error of +/- 3.2 percent, at a 95 percent confidence level.

This first-ever comprehensive, scientific poll of American tastes in art was commissioned by the Russian émigré artists Vitaly Komar and Alexander Melamid in conjunction with The Nation Institute, a non-profit offshoot of The Nation magazine. It was conducted by Martilla & Kiley, Inc., a Boston-based public-opinion research firm …

… [A]ided by international polling firms using variations on the American questionnaire, [they] penetrated Europe, Asia and Africa with their "People's Choice" project … To date, the artists have surveyed the opinions of close to two billion people—almost one-third of the world's population—and have translated the numbers in pictures.

Interview

How did the idea for this poll start?

Alex Melamid: It was a continuation of our works for the last number of years, which was to get in touch with the people of the United States of America: somehow to penetrate their brains, to understand their wishes—to be a real part of this society, of which we're partially part, partially not.

Vitaly Komar: ... [I]t goes back further. I remember our plan to create paintings for different segments of society in Moscow back in 1977. Then, our idea was not associated with poll ... but we were trying to show that Soviet society, in spite of government propaganda, had many contradictions; everyone really was not more or less same socially. Here in America, before we got results of poll, we thought we would have to paint different pictures by income, by race. Instead, we made surprising discovery: in society famous for freedom of expression, freedom of individual, our poll revealed sameness of majority. Having destroyed communism's utopian illusions, we collided with America's virtual reality.

Here, though is another reason behind our polls: the search for new co-authors. Everyone works collaboratively. That is why society exists. Even artist who imagines himself to be like God, a solitary creator, is working in collaboration with his teachers, his predecessors, craftsmen who created his canvas and paints, and so on—just as God created with help of angels. Old romantic view of artist is a travesty of monotheism ...

And now, I would say, conscious co-authorship is only fundamentally new direction in art since discovery of the abstract. Our interpretation of polls is our collaboration with various peoples of the world. It is our collaboration with new dictator—Majority ...

AM: We just were thinking about how this society works, and how the rulers in this society get in touch with the people, with real American people. How producers get in touch with consumers. In real life they take polls. Only recently I discovered that the President has his own pollsters, who work on polls every minute. It's a constant poll of the people. I understand the President very well, because he wants to know as much as me, I suppose, even more. But how to ask? Where are these people? It's a very clumsy tool, this poll, but there's no other tool …

But this idea … of American democracy, is very important … It was really brave and unthinkable break with history, this idea that simple people, innocent people, have some higher rank, are closer to God, are purer than others, and so they should decide….

… [B]ut the problem is that we, the so-called superior people, we ask the questions because we're scared, we're afraid of these people, afraid that we don't understand them. This whole system, American system runs on fear. These people, the masses, are quite powerful, you know, they can be quite powerful, so there's always this threat that if we don't understand them something might happen. Look at Oklahoma City. The point is, whether it's the President of the United States or the artist, there's a border between us and the people. There are some channels for communication between the classes but very few, because socially people are almost totally separate. The rulers base their opinion of the people on statistics, and for the simple people there are society columns, *Vanity Fair*. In fact, even the lower classes get most of their information from statistics, so polls are maybe one of the only means of communication between upper classes and lower classes. And what the poll tells, supposedly, is majority opinion. It might be manipulated or there might be perversions, of course, but still this idea of what is majority opinion is very powerful in American culture. This populist ideal is really important. And in art, we—Vitaly and I—were brought up with the idea that art belongs to the people, and believe me or not, I still believe in this …

You know, the point is maybe the poll is not the best way … But society now depends on polls, so we just pick the tool which is here. And this is scientifically accurate poll, so if this poll is wrong, all polls are wrong. Still, there are some things unknown to me, like it had to be 1,001 persons asked. It needs to be one more than 1,000. I don't know why, but supposedly science tells the pollsters this. But is it real science, or is it a kind of science lite? Since I was always a very bad student in science, I cannot judge this. But that's another story: if you need to have a real truth, or if you just align yourself with what is considered to be the truth here, in this given moment, in this place. So we have this truth—science, medicine, polls—and we say, Okay, that's truth. We trust it. If we don't trust polls, the whole world will collapse. So what to believe? We don't believe in God and we don't believe in science, so what is left …

VK: This is connected with another deep feeling that I believe everybody has. As long as we are mortal, the number of our days, the number of moments in our life, are limited—like money in our account. We pay our moments, our days, for everything … It's the only real money that we have … So when we make paintings, we pay with our life. But in the case of town hall meetings and answering poll questions, the people pay their lives, their moments, for us. We are like vampires; these hundreds, thousands of people who come to these meetings, who talk to pollsters, we suck their blood, their moments …[5]

Notes

1 Honoré de Balzac, *The Physiology of Marriage* [1829] (New York: Albert and Charles Boni, 1925).

2 W. H. Auden, *Collected Poems* (New York, Random House, 1940).

3 Stanislaw Lem, "One Human Minute," *One Human Minute* (New York: Harcourt Brace Jovanovich, 1986).

4 Natalie Jeremijenko, Bureau of Inverse Technology, Suicide Box, www.bureauit.org/sbox.

5 JoAnn Wypijewski, ed., *Painting by Numbers: Komar and Melamid's Scientific Guide to Art* (Berkeley: University of California Press, 1999).

PART II

CYBER PERSONAE

CHAPTER 4

THE CONSUMER'S NEW CLOTHES

Before I begin my attack, I must first become
acquainted with her and her whole mental state.
—Søren Kierkegaard, "A Seducer's Diary" (1843)

Response is the medium!
—Myron Krueger, "Responsive Environments" (1977)

Champions of the public interest praise the Web, at least
in part, because putting communications power in the hands of
consumers helps counterbalance the power of marketers. This
view contains several truths, to be acknowledged in a bit, but
the view of the Web as a weapon in an adversarial relationship is
wrong. Once upon a time, when the Internet was just expanding beyond research universities and government laboratories,
many were opposed to its commercialization. That lasted about
two seconds. Ever since, much of its growth has been based
squarely on its facilitating our shopping and buying.

Tomorrow's Web services will enable us as consumers
even more. New interfaces will enable each of us to manage which parts of our personal information we'll share with
which merchants and even to "advertise" our needs and
wants to them. Consumers will likely interpret this enable-
ment as empowerment and embrace it. If so, our voluntary
self-disclosure will save businesses billions and even help
solve the privacy problem, but we won't get paid or praised

for either. More likely, our machine form as a "virtual con-sumer" will emerge as just another step in the march of cyber-progress, and precisely because some version of a user-managed virtual consumer interface will likely be a standard component of everyone's emerging cyberpersona, it merits close attention. Before doing so, however, the balance-of-power argument needs to be addressed.

The truths of that argument can be quickly acknowl-edged. The Web certainly provides buyers with more perfect information. Attributes and features of every product in ev-ery category are easily located as well as comparative prices and independent product reviews on most of them, which threw businesses into a tizzy for a bit. It also gives irate cus-tomers a very powerful platform for airing grievances, and they do use it. Recently, an audio recording of an AOL call center agent fighting off a subscriber's attempt to cancel spread like wildfire online; so, too, did a video showing how to pick a high-priced Kryptonite bike lock with the back end of a Bic pen. IPhone fans lit up the blogosphere when the steep price they proudly paid at launch was slashed by 30 percent just two months later. Moreover, the Web makes it easier for activists from anywhere to access financial filings, pollution records, political donations, legal briefs and other documents, and their reports of bad deeds or even hypoc-risy also diffuse quickly. The enviro-active soap-peddler The Body Shop, for example, lost some of its luster over allegedly inhumane animal testing, and esteem for organic grocer Whole Foods dipped when its CEO was discovered blogging about his company under an alias.

Businesses have not been idle in responding to these chal-lenges. They use a variety of new tools to monitor, gather and analyze user-generated content (UGC) from across the Web to find out who's talking with whom about what, what they're saying and which users are "hubs," who refer people with questions to "authorities," people who respond with answers. To better understand these conversations, many businesses also use text-processing software that turns the natural language in which people communicate into a more abstracted language that lends itself to analysis and reporting.[1]

Neither irate customers nor eavesdropping businesses, however, suggest that consumers and marketers have an adversarial relationship. The desire to get even does often motivate the initial airings of complaints, but that's not why they diffuse. Offline and on-, we share negative information more widely than we do positive and for the same reasons: we remember the former more often than the latter, and we believe that preventing potential harm is a *bona fide* good deed.[2] Similarly, when it comes to hypocrisy, surely all consumers would advise marketers to follow the Socratic chestnut: Be as you wish to appear. But that does not mean, as some gurus argue, that consumers are clamoring for authenticity.

The Charm of Humbug

When it comes to advertising, consumers are of two minds about veracity because advertising has two functions: information and entertainment.[3] In its informational mode, advertising assumes the consumer is a rational agent, seeking to maximize her interest through the pursuit of calculable benefits. Such calculation requires accurate information and in that context misinformation is problematic. It was a notorious problem in the late 19th century, especially among patent medicine companies with their promise-the-moon claims. In 1913 the advertising industry, long critical of such practices, finally took its stand, adopting the Baltimore Truth Agreement and committing to "Truth in Advertising," which later became the slogan of the Advertising Federation of America and its affiliates.

Since then, we have enacted and still want laws upholding truth in advertising as well as in packaging, labeling, installment buying and other commercial practices. Every buyer wants the product as described, a fair price and an honest tradesman. Indeed, our ethical sense extends beyond what's legally required and makes us uncomfortable with those advertisers who tell the whole truth about their products only in the fine print, such as student-loan originators, debt consolidators and accident claims companies. By and large, however, the advertising industry has lived up to its credo and, miscreants notwithstanding, rarely lies about products.

Veracity is not what we want from advertising's entertainment dimension, however. Americans in particular have always been fond of bold liars and their tall tales, fish stories and other whoppers. Back in the mid-19th century, at the very time patent-medicine companies were peddling their snake-oil cure-alls, Americans adored P. T. Barnum, the self-crowned "prince of humbug," and we crowded his exhibit halls of educated dogs, industrious fleas, automatons, ventriloquists, living statuary, tableaux, gypsies, Albinos, fat boys, giants, dwarfs and outrageous fakes like George Washington's nurse, the Missing Link and a mermaid. The last was a preserved monkey head sewn onto a dried fish, and Barnum recalled how the public reacted to the difference between what he advertised outside the exhibit hall and what it found within:

> The public appeared to be satisfied but as some persons always will take things literally, and make no allowance for poetic license even in mermaids, an occasional visitor, after having seen the large transparency in front of the hall ... would be slightly surprised to find that the reality was a black-looking specimen of dried monkey and fish that a boy a few years old could easily run away with under his arm.[4]

The showman's autobiography was a best seller in his own lifetime.

Fast-forward to the 1980s when ad agency Della Femina, Travisano and Partners created for Isuzu automobiles a spokesperson in the huckster tradition, played with lounge lizard smarm by David Leasure. Across various TV spots,

Joe Isuzu claimed the car gets 94 miles per gallon, city; goes from Paris to Rome in two minutes and has a built-in frozen yogurt machine. Isuzu's pick-up, according to Joe, can haul a 2,000-pound cheeseburger and has more seats than the Astrodome.   And he always exited on the line, "You have my word on it." Whether or not this campaign sold cars, people loved the commercials. And although few campaigns are so extreme, tongue-in-cheek parodies are a staple of the genre, like the current campaigns for Axe men's grooming products and William Shatner's portrayal of the Negotiator for Priceline.

We laugh at marketers' hyperbole and have done so for ages. The 1920s college humor magazine *Ballyhoo* was devoted entirely to satirizing advertising, and by the 1950s parodies had become a regular feature of popular culture from the send-ups in *Mad Magazine* to the actual radio and TV spots created by Stan Freberg. Consumers know enter-tainment when they see it, in advertising as in mermaids, and willingly suspend their disbelief for the sake of their own en-tertainment.[5]

Nor are we fooled by fakery. We don't need warnings that *The Daily Show with Jon Stewart* and "Weekend Update" on *Saturday Night Live* are fake newscasts. No one thinks his city's House of Blues club with its *faux* water damage, graffiti and tobacco stains is actually a Southern juke joint. Everyone knows Restoration Hardware sells reproductions and that the entire knock-off sector of the women's apparel industry is based on the "real fake" and its benefit—looking *a la mode* at a fraction of the designer's price. A few years ago, an up-market Italian home furnishings company commissioned a noted architect to design a teakettle and priced it at $145; a hip discount retailer then commissioned the same architect to design a replica, priced at $25. Both sold well and no one mistook the one for the other.

Nor are consumers out to get marketers. Current re-search reveals that online product reviews are second only to word of mouth in influencing product decisions,[6] and those reviewers are overwhelmingly positive and well intentioned. According to a 2007 survey of 1,300 online reviewers by the Kay Feller Group for Bazaarvoice, a leading consumer review site, 87 percent of all product reviews were generally positive in tone as were the motives for writing them.

- 90 percent to help other consumers make better buying decisions
- 79 percent to reward a company
- 79 percent as a way of giving back to the review community
- 70 percent to help companies improve the products they build and carry.[7]

These consumers don't see marketers as adversaries or the Web as a weapon. They're active online to be helpful, even collaborative. The very success of the Web shows that consumers do much more than meet marketers halfway; with control at our fingertips, we now go to them.

To be sure the Web provides a bullhorn for irate customers and a combination of telescope and microscope for business watchdogs. Louder voices and prying eyes prying more often demand that businesses do more, especially in customer service and stakeholder relations, but not anything different. Meanwhile, the previously mentioned reversal in the direction of communication, from consumers to marketers, is a qualitative change. It inverts the relationship of consumers and marketers and, looking ahead, is inspiring the new virtual-consumer interfaces of our emerging cyberpersonas.

The Inversion of Marketing

For its entire history before the Internet, marketing had always initiated the communication. Online, however, marketers are on the receiving end; the consumer comes to them, usually with intentions in mind and control at her fingertips. This inversion is the path on which marketers are leading us today, but it took a while for them to acknowledge the situation, much less figure out a way to adapt.

When the Web arrived in the mid-1990s, most brands weren't interested. Its early users were too few and elite: they had twice the wealth of the average U.S. household and twice as many college graduates as the U.S. population, and were heavily concentrated in managerial, professional, technical and academic jobs. That market segment did attract some spending from big-ticket categories like automobiles and categories like financial services where customers had high lifetime value, but other categories held back. Ad agencies weren't interested, either; digital didn't pay. In 1997 Internet advertising totaled a mere $200 million, a tiny amount from which all had to make their commissions, while the fees that agencies could charge for producing Web sites and banner ads were equally miniscule. A few traditional agencies did set up digital studios but largely to deter their clients from meeting other agencies.

As Web usage spread and its users came to resemble the general population, more brands in more categories upped their online budgets. But when their agencies tried to implement, they flopped. Their creative departments, the core competency of every agency, didn't like Web work. It wasn't as much fun as shooting a 30-second spot starring a six-foot supermodel. Nor would it advance a career like a Super Bowl spot would. But the best reason agencies' creative staffs didn't like digital work was that they weren't any good at it. And they still aren't.

Admitting so took years, but it finally became clear that one-way and two-way media require different types of creativity. An advertisement is a mini-entertainment, designed to stimulate audiences into reverie. An interface, even the simplest like an ATM, is designed to enable action and response between human and machine. The locus of creativity in interactive media is different, as computer scientist and virtual reality pioneer Myron Krueger explained:

> The medium is comprised of sensing, display and control systems. It accepts inputs from or about the participant and then outputs in a way he can recognize as corresponding to his behavior. The relationship between inputs and outputs is arbitrary and variable, allowing the artist to intervene between the participant's action and the results perceived ... It is the composition of those relationships between action and response that is important ... Response is the medium! [8]

Choreographing a *pas de deux* for human and machine occurs on dimensions that do not even exist in narrative storytelling—feedback, control and adaptivity—and aims at an entirely different result, not reverie but agency, the pleasure of participating in a world that responds coherently to our participation and that changes at our intervention. In this back-and-forth, the user is in control at every step from start to finish, entering commands to which the machine responds. On the Web, for example, a user's click commands the destination site to serve up the requested page; after responding, it stops. Perhaps the user will enter another command, perhaps not.

Adapting to this medium is like a sex change for marketers. Traditional outbound marketing is conceived as a rather aggressive endeavor, in such terms as *targeting, capturing* and *penetrating*. On the Web marketers are on the receiving end, responding to users coming to them, and their success depends on embracing the inbound visitor through a new set of abilities: seducing, engaging, listening and adapting. Of course, putting a gender spin on this is cheesy, but others have also flirted with this metaphor because it helps convey the profound nature of the inversion the new digital media require.[9]

At the risk of being extra cheesy, the metaphor plays out as follows. While Mr. Advertisement fills up the time slot or print lineage with his words, sounds and images, Ms. Web site offers space that the visitor fills up with inputs, usually by making choices or entering data. Open to entrance, she pulls the visitor in and along, by laying out sequences of steps for her visitors to follow that guide the intentions that prompted their visits to successful conclusions. Since the visitor holds the mouse, every step must be designed not to sell but to help the visitor buy. Ms. Web also listens and adapts. If the user reveals a bit, she'll change herself a bit to reflect what she's learned; the more the user reveals, the more she'll adapt. The seductress, inviting, open to entrance and responsive, is the muse of effective Web design.[10]

A real-world shift in technical metaphors, less fun of course, also captures the reversal: Computer Human Interface (CHI) design became Human Computer Interaction (HCI) design. Similarly, interface design, which emphasized the presentation of information, was replaced by interaction design, which emphasizes user-experience dimensions such as usability, flow and persuasion.[11] This approach, generally called user-centric design (UCD), is almost universal today and widely applauded for empowering consumers. Specifically, the elusive object of marketers' desires in the offline world is transformed on the Web into an approaching subject who has intentions and control, and the burden is on marketers to respond to her. Such empowerment sounds fine, but it does assume and require voluntary self-disclosure from the *U* in *UCD*.

Quite literally, UCD tries to get inside users' heads by deconstructing our consideration paths and decision processes and then mapping them into the command-and-response sequences of the software. Of course, visitors' heads are different, even for the same product. For example, buying life insurance for family protection is a different decision than buying it for estate planning. So, interaction designers must envision various personas (fictitious types of persons) by asking such questions as, What different product benefits do they seek? What are their different barriers, resources and expectations? Which tasks of their considering can the interface enable? What answers will convert their considerations into a purchase decision? With answers in hand, whether researched or hypothesized, designers then map these consideration paths and decision processes into flow charts that specify what content and what tools are needed at each click along the personas' different but partially overlapping and intersecting journeys through the site.

To clarify what designers do and users never see, Krueger offered a musical analogy: the designer is the composer, the software is the score and the user is the performer. The composer doesn't know in advance which performer will play on any given day and, so, must compose a score containing multiple sequences of alternative possibilities, most of which will not be realized by any given performer.[12] Because each click is a choice that reveals the visitor's intention at the moment and is recorded on the site's server logs as a visitor-specific clickstream, close monitoring of visitor behavior informs the site's next iteration. That is, by analyzing visitors' clickstreams, user-centric designers learn which pathways, content and tools worked and which didn't for which persona—in short, how we consider and decide—and adjust the site's pathways, content and tools accordingly.

UCD is a real achievement. It implements the inversion in the direction of communications and has proved its effectiveness in e-commerce. A secondary but still substantial benefit to business, the data it collects is high quality on several dimensions. Captured in real time during Web sessions, it cannot be surpassed for recency. Driven by user intentions and actions, the data are salient and relevant on the category, brand and product levels. Moreover, depending on the paths visitors are led down, their data can reveal interests, tastes, curiosities and other personal details. Whether or not a Web site is like a woman, it's the visitors who are taking off their clothes.

Birthing the Virtual Consumer

Beyond UCD the next step in consumer empowerment is a big one. It envisions equipping consumers with a user-managed interface that enables each to manage, update and selectively disclose different digital versions of themselves to different marketers. Two independent but complementary initiatives—one at Harvard, the other at Microsoft—are pioneering our virtual-consumer interfaces.

The work at Harvard's Berkman Center for Internet and Society on vendor relationship management (VRM) is led by Doc Searls, whose pedigree helps explain the consumerist values behind the project. Ten years ago, he co-authored *The Cluetrain Manifesto*, a controversial best seller that challenged businesses to take advantage of the Web's inbound communication path by doing a lot more listening to customers.[13] The book's confrontational tone was entirely merited by business' widespread indifference to this unprecedented opportunity. In the years since businesses have come around; they've become increasingly comfortable with customers who talk to them and are even learning how to actively listen.

Recent efforts aim to get customers inside the enterprise, as far upstream as product development, where companies and customers can create products collaboratively.[14] Some "advanced" customers are especially worth listening to, including lead customers, who know the product itself inside and out; product enthusiasts, who know how to use the product better than others do and early adopters, who must have whatever is the latest and greatest.

Although this practice began in the high-tech industry, it's become a best practice in many categories. Packaged goods giant Procter & Gamble (P&G) is an exemplary exponent and explained its own shift quite simply: "We were the biggest shouter in the 20th century. In the 21st century, we want to be the best listener."[15]   It revamped its Web site and invited all visitors "to see and share ideas for improving our brands and creating new ones," "to get free samples and buy our latest innovations before they hit the store shelves," and to "tell us what you think about" different P&G products. Another P&G initiative, an effort to engage online with opinion leaders among teenage girls, was spun off into its own marketing company. Today, leading companies in many categories are increasingly engaged in *preferential* listening with all three advanced customer groups.

Of course, listening has limits. The market research industry quickly pointed out that advanced customers are not representative and, furthermore, that the voluntarism of any self-selecting group is itself a bias that randomly selected samples avoid. It is certainly true that online market research has serious methodological challenges but some of this reaction was defensive.[16] The industry stands on its ability to generalize reliably from a sample to a population, but as discussed earlier, counting is not listening. Indeed, the isolated and transient relationship between researcher and respondent may allow only counting; research may be unable to listen.

Others rightly note that customers are limited in what they can contribute. When asked about existing products, they tend to suggest incremental improvements of what they already know, and when given a clean slate, they can't envision what new products they might want. No customer could envision Post-it notes, Velcro or the microwave oven. Still others put listening in context: it's only one element in being a customer-centric company.[17] Finally, it also has some dangers, such as disputes over intellectual property, arguments over product direction and tendencies toward feature creep and over-specialization in product design.[18]

Nevertheless, preferential listening is likely to expand since it also strengthens customer relationships, generates referrals, engages employees and reduces service costs[19] while counterbalancing organizational inertia and resistance to innovation.[20] It's also becoming easier and cheaper. As more companies connect with their customers via technology, they're using those IT systems to hardwire the voice of the customer into their organizations.[21]

The Cluetrainers were right—the Web can empower customers to the benefit of business—and that same vision informs Searls' Harvard work. Indeed, ProjectVRM rejects the term *user-centric* as inadequate and substitutes *user-driven* to describe the level of control needed for consumers to be-come "independent leaders and not just captive followers in their relationships with vendors."[22] That's the ideal, as Searls explained on the project's blog. "Our logic ... starts with the sovereign autonomy and independence of each individual as a fully-empowered participant in the relationships that com-prise markets and other social arrangements."[23]

In a VRM solution, "fully empowered" means that the consumer has both content and control of that content's disclosure. Specifically, she would have all the behavioral data relevant to each brand, retailer or other vendor from whom she buys, including her transaction histories, service records and correspondence, as well as her expressed data, such as purchase intentions and brand preferences. Most important, she'd have the ability to decide which data sets to share with which vendors and on what terms, like once-only use, anonymous use and so on. The benefit promised in the short term is the ability to automate some of our tasks as con-sumers, such as researching a big-ticket purchase, renewing subscriptions and policies and scheduling routine service ap-pointments, but the longer-term ambition is grander.

VRM proponents envision and hope to enable "pro-fessionalized" consumers, who will gather, store, protect, analyze and share information describing themselves, their relationships, transactions and intentions and on that basis improve their abilities to plan, administer, organize and con-duct their interactions and transactions with vendors. In the VRM future, consumers will be data-mining our own records of our personal spending, calorie intake, energy usage and car mileage, modeling our own profiles and constructing our own "people like me" comparisons in order to discover how we can better anticipate our needs, manage our resources and make better buying decisions.

The star of the VRM solution is the consumer who "ad-vertises" her needs and wants to marketers. In what Searls calls The Intention Economy, "the buyer notifies the mar-ket of the intent to buy, and sellers compete for the buyer's purchase."[24] Some online vendors, such as Lending Tree and Priceline, already do this. The consumer posts her requirements and receives corresponding offers from marketers. With a VRM solution, consumers would expose the needs they want met across many categories. That's only fair, according to ProjectVRM. Since it "is impossible for vendor-side CRM systems to bear the full burden of relating with customers, … there should be a way for the customers to bear some of that weight."[25] As *Wired* editor Kevin Kelly predicted, "In network economics the customer can expect increasing speed and choice, and more responsibility as a customer."[26]

Microsoft's version of the virtual-consumer interface, Windows Card Space (née InfoCard) is similarly user-driven, but its goal is to create a Web-wide e-wallet and its rationale for its design decisions has none of ProjectVRM's idealism.[27] Graphically, each of the user's merchant relationships is represented as an ID card. For example, a hotel-branded card identifies the user as a preferred guest, an online bank card identifies the user as having a checking account and an auto loan and so forth. The user updates, verifies and controls each card, and each card contains only that subset of user data required for that specific merchant, including the purposes for which and contexts in which it can be used. Technically, the solution enables users to manage two security procedures: authorization that controls access and authentication that verifies identity. Specifically, the consumer both authorizes different merchants to access different subsets of her data and manages her own authentication so transactions can proceed.

This user-managed approach reverses the approach the software giant took with *Hailstorm*. That earlier effort at a Web-wide e-wallet was centralized with Microsoft at the center, storing all consumer data and interfacing with all merchants. It flopped because consumers wouldn't entrust all their identity data to a single organization, because merchants saw no reason for a middleman between them and their customers and because no single identity system would work everywhere.

In contrast Windows CardSpace uses a distributed approach, pushing control and responsibility out to the end users.

User control is preeminent. It's the first and foremost of Microsoft's "Laws of Identity," but the rationale is pure *realpolitik*. Specifically, a large enough minority of consumers would reject a solution that did not offer user control and thereby deny Microsoft the universality it seeks. As explained by Microsoft identity architect Kim Cameron, the goal is to establish a technical standard that works for everyone everywhere and ideals have nothing to do with it:

> When we postulate the Law of User Control ... it is because experience tells us: a system that does not put users in control will—immediately or over time—be rejected by enough of them that it cannot *become and remain* a unifying technology. How this law meshes with values is not the relevant issue.[28]

Microsoft's second law of identity is "minimal disclosure for a constrained use"[29] and its goal is similarly pragmatic: disclosing less and imposing limits on disclosures decrease risk. For example, when asking a user to indicate his age, offering a set of age ranges, such as under 18, 18—24, 25   31, and so on, is less risky than asking for a date of birth from which a real-life person could be identified. Protecting privacy is an unintended consequence; risk mitigation is the goal.[30] (Microsoft's other "laws" concern the architecture of a distributed identity/authorization system so it works optimally across multiple contexts for all justified parties.)

Although ProjectVRM is governed by ideals and Microsoft by *realpolitik*, both net out in the same place and lead in the same direction: toward a user-managed interface running on Web-wide platforms that enable each of us to identify, authenticate and manage our self-disclosure to marketers and their agencies. This future is almost a certainty because the benefit to business is so substantial. Currently, the supply side tries to predict who on the demand side wants and needs what when. If marketers could replace their data-crunching guesswork with our voluntary and selective disclosure of purchase-relevant information, that is, if each of us were to become our own consumer-to-business (C2B) marketer and "advertise" our intentions to sellers, they would save billions. In contrast to the attention economy where traditional marketing does its work, in the intention economy consumers do the work. If that's accurate, the producers of intentions should get paid.

Consumers know their personal information has value. In 2006 personal-finance columnist Dave Ramsey revealed to readers of *Quick & Simple*, a weekly magazine from Hearst Communication, the then-current prices for a few of our many and varied data bits:

Bankruptcy details	$26.50
Workers' Comp history	$18.00
Unpublished phone number	$17.50
Cell phone number	$10.00
Social Security number	$8.00
Date of birth	$2.00
Street address	$0.50

He suggested consumers ask for a piece of the action.[31] Some have tried.

A London designer put up for sale on eBay 800 pieces of personal information; he got the equivalent of $240. Similarly, an office manager in Madison, Wisconsin, offered 378 of her data points, including her health status and religious beliefs. Another seller, identified by the moniker "highlytargeted," auctioned off a package of information "to help you better target ads to me." It included the past 30 days of her Internet search queries, the past 90 days of her Web surfing history and the past 30 days of her on- and offline purchase activity, as well as age, gender, ethnicity, marital status and geographic location, plus the right to target her with one commercial e-mail per day for 30 days. Another proposed to sell his "intention to buy" data for the next six months, broken down by category, likely purchase dates, indicative price ranges and existing preferences of various types, packaged in a format that feeds straight into CRM systems and priced at £10 per category for one- off use. He guaranteed that his data "will be more predictive of what I'm going to buy than your own analysis or what you can buy from external data providers.[32]

A marketplace in personal information is not a far-fetched notion to John Deighton, a professor at Harvard Business School:

> The challenge is to give people a claim on their identities while protecting them from mistreatment. The solution is to create institutions that allow consumers to build and claim the value of their marketplace identities and that give producers the incentive to respect them. Privacy and identity then become opposing economic goods, and consumers can choose how much of each they would like.[33]

The economics should work. Product information from marketers is in big supply; it has low value to consumers and is given away for free. Conversely, consumer information from individuals is in short supply; it should have high value for businesses and could pay out for the individual. What individual-level data could we sell that marketers don't already have? We could sell our online attention data (a.k.a., surfing histories or "clickstreams"), which could include the sites and blogs we visit; the time of day we visited and how long we stayed; what we read, watched, listened to, downloaded, shared, linked to or wrote about; where we had come from before and where we went after.[34] We could sell our taste data, expressed in the favorite books, movies, TV programs, music and quotations that highlight our profiles on social networking sites or expressed in behavior-based data, such as books bought, tickets purchased, songs listened to, feeds subscribed to and many others. We could sell our purchase

intentions, which could include category, product specifica-
tions, price range, brand preferences and likely purchase
dates. The more specific, up-to-date and complete our
self-disclosure, the more valuable it would be, and, if it includes authenticated and/or audited data, its value would
increase even further.[35]

Unfortunately for consumers, the law is not on our side.
U.S. case law has largely limited property rights in one's likeness and the right of publicity—to own, protect and commercially exploit one's name and likeness—to celebrities. Their
likenesses are complete and generally recognizable, the law
argues. The same cannot be said of our purposefully partial
and ephemeral profiles in the datascape, but it could be said
of the user-managed interfaces that present us as virtual consumers.

As for our property rights in the data we generate, the
courts ruled that the data has no value. Rather, the value derives from and resides with the information companies that
compile and categorize the raw data into databases. This
created a logical inconsistency. Since these companies are
not alchemists, the value of the data they aggregate cannot be zero. Accordingly, some legal scholars have argued
that the value of the raw data is determined by how much
it takes for a person to relinquish it. Since millions of us
readily give up our information for product coupons, ringtones, screen savers, horoscopes and other trifles, its value to
us must be low, they argue, and they conclude that we're already adequately compensated by the marketplace.[36] No one
believes that, and some have suggested that the law could
support payment for information if privacy notices were
replaced by a contract between consumer and merchant
governing the data exchange, enforceable under existing
contract law.

Perhaps the day is just around the corner when consumers will be able to disintermediate both the data industry and
the media and monetize for themselves the information that
is by and about them. The technological solutions are al-

ready in development, the economics are right, the law could work and the consumer is ready. As Internet venture capitalist Fred Wilson noted, "People are starting to get used to profiling themselves and using it to add value to their Internet experience ... That change in user behavior is a big deal."[37]

Indeed, tens of millions of us are already busy disclosing ourselves in intimate detail on social network sites, blogs and other Web 2.0 services. Moreover, as more of our everyday activities take place or get captured online, each of us is accumulating an even larger online presence that others use to get acquainted with and evaluate us. The user-managed virtual consumer is but one component of everyone's emerging cyberpersona. Building, managing and governing access to one's online presence is an inescapable future that each of us must also address.

Notes

1 For a review of conversation monitoring services, see www.rmmlondon.com/rchive/a-survey-of-ten-leading-online-conversation-monitoring-companies

2 Pete Blackshaw, *Satisfied Customers Tell Three Friends, Angry Customers Tell 3,000: Running a Business in Today's Consumer-Driven World* (New York: Broadway Business, 2008) is a cogent assessment of the current scene. The groundbreaking study of word of mouth is Elihu Katz and Paul F. Lazarsfeld, *Personal Influence* (New York: The Free Press, 1955). On negative word of mouth see Robert J. Bies and Thomas M. Tripp, "Beyond Distrust: 'Getting Even' and the Need for Revenge," in R.M. Kramer and T.R. Tyler, eds. *Trust in Organizations: Frontiers of Theory and Research* (Thousand Oaks, CA: Sage, 1996), 246—260, and the two pioneering studies Marc G. Weinberger, Chris T. Allen and William R. Dillon, "Negative Information: Perspectives and Research Directions," 390—404 and Carol K. Scott and Alice M. Tybout, "Theoretical Perspectives on

the Impact of Negative Information," 408—409, both in *Advances in Consumer Research*, vol. 8, ed. Kent B. Munroe (Ann Arbor: Association for Consumer Research, 1981).

3 It is generally believed that advertising was largely informational in the 19th century and became increasingly focused on entertainment over the course of the 20th century, but the historical record on this matter is inconclusive; see Schudson, 59—64.

4 Daniel J. Boorstin, *The Image: A Guide to Pseudo-Events in America* (New York: Harper & Row, 1961), 207—210 discusses Barnum and is the source of this quotation.

5 On the mixture of tolerance and skepticism with which consumers approach advertising, see Schudson, 108—111.

6 Bruce LaFeetra, "Online Reviews Second Only to Word of Mouth as Purchase Influencer in US," Rubicon Consulting, October 2008, http://rubiconculting.com/ insight/ whitepapers/2008/10/online reviews-second-only-to.html. The reach and influence of bloggers in purchase consideration is still evolving; see "Blog Influence on Consumer Purchases Eclipses Social Networks," BuzzBlog, October 28, 2008, www.buzzlogic.com/2008/10/28/blog-influence-on-consumer-purchases-eclipses-social networks.

7 "Keller Fay Group and Bazaarvoice Study Finds Altruism Drives Online Reviewers," Bazaarvoice, November 26, 2007, www.bazaarvoice.com/resources/press-room/us-press-room/190-pressrelease phpid18?q=keller+fay+group

8 Myron W. Krueger, "Responsive Environments," in Noah Wardrip-Fruin and Nick Montfort, eds., *The New Media Reader* (Cambridge, MA: The MIT Press, 2003), 379—389. This weakness was not due to the lack of technical skills. Ten years ago, the CEO of a Fortune 100 company in an issue-sensitive industry was tired of getting beaten up by some stakeholder group—unions, regulators, activists, trading partners, equity analysts—every time the company did

anything. To highlight this situation, its digital agency designed a game for the corporation's Web site that dared visitors to sit in the CEO's "hot seat" and respond to a hypothetical scenario-of-the-week by reviewing and selecting one of five options. But every option the visitor selected just brought a blast of vehement and credible objections from one or more of the hypothetical stakeholder groups. There was no right answer, ever. This no-win game was a hands-on experience of the client's dilemma but, technically, it was just HTML pages.

9 See Nathan Shedroff, *Experience Design* (Indianapolis: New Riders, 2001); Mark C. Taylor and Esa Saarinen, *Imagologies: Media Philosophy* (New York: Routledge, 1994); John R. Patrick, *Net Attitude: What It Is, How to Get It, and Why Your Company Can't Survive Without It* (Cambridge, MA: Perseus, 2001) and Lena Waters, "E-mail life cycle: from dating to divorce," *DM News,* July 10, 2007.

10 For similar reasons marketers have had a hard time hosting online communities. The trick is conceiving empty space as a generative field. Letting others do the talking, moderating their conversation only to ensure its continued benefit to the participants and being a center of gravity for others without being the center of attention have proven hard for most marketers.

11 Usability and its goal of intuitive instrumentality is championed most notably by Jakob Nielsen, *Usability Engineering* (San Francisco: Morgan Kaufmann, 1993) and his narrower *Designing Web Usability* (Berkeley: Peachpit Press, 1999). Mihaly Csíkszentmihályi, *Flow: The Psychology of Optimal Experience* (New York: Harper and Row, 1990) is the seminal text on flow and its attributes—attention, immersion and success. An early examination of flow's role in Web design with an emphasis on its implications for marketers is Donna L. Hoffman and Thomas P. Novak, "Marketing in Hypermedia Computer-Mediated Environments," Working Paper no. 1 (July 1995), Research Program on Marketing in Computer-Mediated Environments, Owen Graduate School of Management, Vanderbilt University. On persuasion, see B. J. Fogg *Persuasive Technology:*

Using Computers to Change What We Think and Do (San Francisco: Morgan Kaufmann Publishers, 2002) and the Stamford University Persuasive Technology Lab at http://captology.stanford.edu. Stuart K. Card, Thomas P. Moran and Allen Newell, *The Psychology of Human–Computer Interaction* (Mahwah, NJ: Lawrence Erlbaum Associates, 1983) is the foundational text of the larger field.

12 Web design must also accommodate the different ways in which companies qualify leads, customize and bundle products, fulfill orders and service customers.

13 Rick Levine, Christopher Locke, Doc Searls and David Weinberger, *The Cluetrain Manifesto: The End of Business as Usual* (Cambridge, MA: Perseus Books, 1999).

14 C. K. Prahalad and Venkat Ramaswamy, *The Future of Competition: Co-creating Unique Value with Customers* (Cambridge, MA: Harvard Business School Press, 2004); Scott Cook, "The Contribution Revolution: Letting Volunteers Build Your Business," *Harvard Business Review* (October 2008) and B. Joseph Pine II and James H. Gilmore, *The Experience Economy: Work is Theatre & Every Business a Stage* (Boston: Harvard Business School Press, 1999) explore the collaborative model of creating value. Kevin Kelly, *Out of Control: The New Biology of Machines, Social Systems and the Economic World* (Reading, MA: Addison-Wesley, 1994) and Michael Rothschild, *Bionomics: Economy as Ecosystem* (New York: Henry Holt, 1990) explore a like theme in terms of symbiotic relationships and "co-evolution."

15 Fara Warner, "Don't Shout, Listen," Fast Company, no. 49 (July 2001) at www.fastcompany.com/magazine/49/bestpractice.html.

16 See Joe Mandese, "Research Pros Concerned About Online Surveys, Recommend Solutions, *Online Media Daily*, May 7, 2007; Jack Neff, "The End of Consumer Surveys? P&G, Unilever Join ARF in Effort to Move Beyond Question-and-Answer," *AdAge* September 15, 2008.

17 See Bruce Temkin, *The 6 Laws of Customer Experience: The Fundamental Truths that Define How Organizations Treat Customers,* http://experiencematters.wordpress.com/2008/07/22/free-book-the-6-laws-of-customer-experience. See also Peter Kim with Chris Charron, Jennifer Joseph, Freda Lynn Gates and Elana Anderson, "Reinventing the Marketing Organization," Forrester Research (July 13, 2006).

18 See Anthony W. Ulwick, "Turn Customer Input into Innovation" and Dorothy Leonard, "The Limitations of Listening," both in *Harvard Business Review,* January 2002; Stefan Thomke and Eric Von Hippel, "Customers as Innovators: A New Way to Create Value," *Harvard Business Review,* April 2002 and Alexander Kandybin, "Survival of the Fittest Innovation," *Strategy + Business,* August 5, 2008.

19 James L. Heskett, W. Earl Sasser and Joe Wheeler, *Ownership Quotient: Putting the Service Profit Chain to Work for Unbeatable Competitive Advantage* (Cambridge, MA: Harvard Business School Press, 2008). Also, Scott Cook, "The Contribution Revolution: Letting Volunteers Build Your Business," *Harvard Business Review,* October 2008 and CMO Council, "Giving Customer Voice More Volume" (2009).

20 John Seely Brown, *Seeing Differently: Insights on Innovation* (Cambridge, MA: Harvard Business School Press, 1997); Michael Schrage, "My Customer, My Co-Innovator," *Strategy + Business eNews,* August 31, 2006; "How Companies Turn Customers' Big Ideas into Innovations, *Strategy + Business,* January 12, 2005.

21 Richard Whiteley and Diane Hessan, *Customer-centered Growth: Five Proven Strategies for Building Competitive Advantage* (New York: Basic Books, 1997).

22 "Main Page," ProjectVRM, http://cyberlaw.harvard.edu/projectvrm/Main_Page.

23 Doc Searls, "VRM is user-driven," ProjectVRM Blog, April 28, 2008, http://blogs.law.harvard.edu/vrm/2008/04/28/vrm-is-user-driven. Useful delineations of the ethical issues involved in

information-based marketing can be found in Claire Gauzente and Ashok Rachhod, "Ethical Marketing for Competitive Advantage on the Internet," *Academy of Marketing Science Review*, vol. 2001, no. 10 (2001); George R. Milne, "The effectiveness of self-regulated privacy protection: A review and framework for future research," in *Handbook of Marketing and Society*, Paul N. Bloom and Gregory T. Gundlach, eds. (Thousand Oaks, CA: Sage Publications, 2001) and Margo Buchanan-Oliver and David Redmore, "Trust-Based Customer Information Management (CIM) in the Network Economy: A Strategic Approach" (2002), www.impgroup.org/uuploads/papers/497.pdf.

24 Doc Searls, "Intention Economy Traction," ProjectVRM Blog, November 15, 2009, http://blogs.harvard.edu/vrm/2009/11/15/intention-economy-traction.

25 Doc Searls "Building the Intention Economy," ProjectVRM Blog, September 14, 2008, http://blogs.law.Harvard.edu/vrm/1008/09/14/building-the-intention-economy. In the business-to-business sector of the economy, some purchasing departments have done this for quite some time; they call it pro-active procurement and reverse marketing. See Wim G. Biemans and Maryse J. Brand, *Reverse Marketing: Synergy of Purchasing and Relationship Marketing*, www.crm2day.com/library/docs/ap0001.pdf.

26 Kelly, 201.

27 Windows InfoCard is described in layman's terms at http://technet.microsoft.com/en-us/magazine/cc160966.aspx. and in technical terms at http://msdn.microsoft.com/en-us/library/ms996422.aspx. For the company's aspirations with Hailstorm, see R. Batchelder, D. Smith, T. Bittman, "AOL vs. Microsoft: The Real Prize Is Online Presence," *Gartner Research Note* (February 22, 2002).

28 Kim Cameron, "Laws of Identity," MSDN, http://msdn.Microsoft.com/en-us/library/ms996456.aspx.

29 Ibid.

30 A distributed approach to managing personal information also avoids the near insurmountable difficulties of imposing a regulatory regime on the tens of thousands of database-enabled computers.

31 Reported in "What's Offline," *The New York Times*, (December 9, 2006).

32 See Jane Black, "Wanna See My Personal Data? Pay Up," *Business Week*, November 21, 2002, www.businessweek.com/technology/content/nov2002/tc20021121_8723.htm; Diane Anderson, "Woman Auctions Personal Info Online," *Industry Standard*, June 15, 2000, www.pcworld.com/article/17199/woman_auctions_personal_info_online.html and Iain Henderson, "Can I Own My Data," Right Side Up, October 26, 2007, http://rightsideup.blogs.com/my_Weblog/2007/10/can-i-own-my-da.html. See also Jeff Gates, "Artist Sells Himself on eBay," *Rhizome*, June 1, 1999. For an early effort in this direction, see "It's My Profile," Wayback Machine, http://Web.archive.org/Web/20011129042113/http://www.itsmyprofile.com/.

33 "Selling Your Personal Data: Interview with John Deighton," CNET News.com, September 1, 2003, http://news.cnet.com/2030-1069_3-5068504.html and John Deighton, "Marketing Solutions to Privacy Problems," HBS working paper abstract at www.hbs.edu/research/facpubs/workingpapers/abstracts/0203/03-024.html.

34 The nonprofit Attention Trust has made some efforts in this direction. There's even been work on an Attention Profiling Markup Language that would enable the exchange of various kinds of personal attention data, that is, information about what someone pays attention to; see www.apml.org.

34 U.S. consumers are rather sophisticated about what personal data they would trade for what benefits. According to a 2004 survey,

fewer than one in five see the exchange of demographic information for more relevant advertising to be worthwhile. Double that number, however, would share information about future purchases in exchange for relevance. See "Consumers Are More Willing to Share Purchase Plans Than Demographic Data," *Consumer Technographics August 2004: North American Devices, Marketing, and Media Online Study* (Cambridge, MA: Forrester Research, August, 2004.

36 Patricia Mell, "Seeking Shade in a Land of Perpetual Sunlight: Privacy as Property in the Electronic Wilderness," *Berkeley Technology Law Journal,* vol. 11 (1996), www.law.berkeley.edu/journals/btlj/articles/vol11/Mell.pdf, reviews how U.S. law defines our property rights in our own information.

37 See "The Implicit Web," http://www.avc.com/a_vc/2006/12/2007_the_implic.html.

CHAPTER 5

VIRTUAL ME

How dreary to be somebody!
How public like a frog
To tell one's name the livelong day
To an admiring bog!

—Emily Dickinson, *Poems* (1861)

If you want to communicate, you have to be connected.
And if you are connected, then you are part of a community
that expects to know something about you.

—Geoff Smith, Capgemini (1999)

Everyone has an online presence. Even without ever going online, each of us has what the Pew Internet & American Life Project calls a digital footprint with passive and active parts.[1] The passive part consists of birth certificates, marriage licenses, real estate deeds, court cases, charitable donations and other public records, which any investigative service will find in a few hours for a modest fee. Also included are any other public mentions of one's name, such as being listed as a conference speaker on an organizer's Web site or as a family member at a wedding announced in a local newspaper; any search engine will find those references in a few seconds for free. This part of the footprint is passive because it does not require any deliberate activity by the individual. In contrast, the active part consists of content created and published by the user. That's the part that's recently exploded.

Many people jumped at the chance to publish as soon as the Internet went public. In those text-only early years, people joined Usenet newsgroups and logged on to bulletin board systems, where they read and wrote to each other on every conceivable topic, from diabetes to foot fetishism.[2] When the World Wide Web arrived in 1994, a self-publishing land rush followed the next year. A new site, GeoCities, provided its users with very simple tools to author and publish Web pages about themselves or their businesses, and within two years it had signed up a million "homesteaders."[3]

Today, an expanding variety of second-generation Web, or Web 2.0, applications enable users to create and publish content easily. They're cropping up everywhere.[4] Topic-specific and affinity-based sites provide such tools, encouraging their visitors to coalesce into frequently visited conversational communities. Brand-specific sites do so as well, hoping to deepen relationships with customers and stimulate customer attachment to their brands.[5] Even online media sites, although focused like all media properties on the content they produce, are enabling visitors to chip in.

Amid all this UGC, there are five Web 2.0 services that provide platforms for individuals to build out their own online presence: social network sites like MySpace and Facebook, blogs and microblogs like Twitter, file hosting sites like YouTube for videos and Flickr for photos, social bookmarking sites like Digg and Delicious and reviewer sites like the comprehensive Epinions and the specialized TripAdvisor.[6] This is where tens of millions of us are typing ourselves into cyber-existence.[7] By 2008, over 79 million US Internet users had created their own profiles at social network sites, including half of all teens and one in five adults (aged 18 or older) while between 23 million and 27 million of us (depending on the source) have started our own blogs.[8] Many millions more have taken smaller steps, posting and signing product reviews, sharing and rating music and videos, tagging and commenting on news stories.

Individual motives in this rush to self-publish are already irrelevant because having some form of positive online presence is emerging as a social expectation. According to Pew, 6 percent of U.S. adults, 11 percent of all adult Internet users and 18 percent of working college graduates report that their employers expect some form of online self-marketing as part of the job. Similarly, one in five working US adults (20 percent) say their employer has a policy about how employees present themselves online, including what can and cannot be shared on blogs and elsewhere.[9] Not surprisingly, hiring officers, as many as half according to one 2007 estimate, vet candidates via online searches, and in 2007 almost half of U.S. Internet users (44 percent) checked what recruiters and others found by searching their own name.[10] Being findable and knowable online is extending into our private lives, too. Homebuyers check out their prospective next-door neighbors; hobbyists and volunteers look each other up; singles research their dates, even their live-in partners. Today, the purposeful production and management of one's self-presentation via Web 2.0 services is an asset. Tomorrow, as more of our everyday lives occurs or gets replicated online, this task will likely be inescapable.[11]

The typical advice about presenting ourselves online is schoolmarmish. Rightly, we're told to express ourselves appropriately since whatever we publish is "an advertisement for what you want other people to know and remember about you." It's also true that the more personal information we share, the more vulnerable we are to scams, spam and identity theft. Finally, everyone really should remember that the Internet is a permanent record. Deleting something doesn't make it disappear, since anything published online could have been viewed, e-mailed, printed or archived by almost anyone else.

While sound, these cautions are misleading. They point toward privacy, toward withholding oneself from view. The worriers are missing the opportunity that beckons from the other direction—advancing oneself into view. Exposing and promoting one's personality in public has traditionally been the preserve of entertainers, athletes, some debutantes and other headline-grabbers. Going forward, it's for everyone and rather than shrink from it, we should embrace it according to cyber-sociologist and blogger danah m. boyd [sic]:

> Carefully crafting and cautiously managing one's public image is a critical aspect of living in a mediated public world. Every advice column I've read warns people of the dangers of living online. I think that this is idiotic. People need to embrace the world we live in and learn to work within its framework. Don't panic about being public—embrace it and handle it with elegance.[12]

Understanding how Web 2.0 services shape our self-presentation in different ways has pragmatic benefits for this task but before exploring those specifics, two features of the entire terrain should be introduced.

First, becoming visible via these services has two dimensions—quantitative and qualitative, one's presence and reputation, respectively. Presence refers to the volume of online content, both *about* the individual (passive) and *by* the individual (active). Reputation refers to what others think about the quality of that content, expressed explicitly by their ratings of and implicitly by their linking to that content. (Reputation can have consequences. For example, search engines count the number of links going to a piece of content as the measure of its authority; the more links the content gets, the higher it's ranked on the search engine results page.) One can build one's presence by contributing content, but one must earn one's reputation from others, when they rate that content highly or insert links to it.

The second feature of the Web 2.0 terrain is that self-presentation occurs with and co-depends on others. Indeed, many Web 2.0 applications are referred to as "social media" because they enable users converse with and link to each other. Both one's presence and reputation are first and fore-most the patterns of these connections: *You are whom you net-work with, how often you share, whom you link to and who links to you.* In short, the post-human version of us in the Web 2.0 world is a network effect.

Social Network Sites

On social network sites (SNSs) each of us is the star of our own social system. These sites assume that the self is a social entity, that the individual and her network go together, and all enable both self-presentation and the connections with whom to share it. In concrete terms, a new user begins by filing out a form that asks for individually descriptive in-formation and by uploading one or more photos; the answers and images are then published on a preformatted page as the user's profile. Once the self-portrait is in place, the user invites other users whom she already knows from real life—relatives, friends, coworkers, classmates—to link their pro-files, creating a network of *friends, fans, contacts* or other term for these connections.[13] In addition to these "strong ties" of our everyday lives, these networks can also include our "weak ties," such as a person met at a conference, a former teacher or a fellow hobbyist; indeed, the ability to maintain our weak ties more easily may constitute the SNSs' novel contribution to social life.[14] In any case, each of us is the center of our own small world on this Web 2.0 platform.

Consumer SNSs such as Facebook and MySpace and business SNSs such as LinkedIn and Plaxo realize this basic structure in different ways. A Facebook profile includes age, gender, location, interests and hobbies, plus favorite movies, books and quotes because its purpose is to convey what the user is like as a person. A LinkedIn profile is largely a ré-sumé; it includes work history, expertise and education be-cause its purpose is to convey how the profile owner can be useful to her business network—employers, clients, partners or other business entities.

Other features line up behind these basic purposes. Facebook friends can "scrawl" messages on a "wall" on the profile owner's page; LinkedIn connections can write references for other LinkedIn users whom they know as current or former coworkers, supervisors and clients. Facebook users can create whatever groups suit their interests. LinkedIn users can create groups, too. Early on, groups were limited to a few pre-set categories: one's *alma mater*, current employer, former employer and professional associations; recently, the site adopted a more liberal policy. Facebook makes it easy for users to connect with friends, their friends' friends and so on. On LinkedIn in contrast the user's connections are categorized as direct, once removed and twice removed, and using those connections to meet someone new requires personal referrals at every step. Such differences align with our personal and professional purposes, and many people create profiles at multiple SNSs.[15] (I have profiles at Facebook and LinkedIn.)

As we fulfill our purposes on SNSs, we also fulfill the SNSs purposes—to sell our eyeballs to advertisers. LinkedIn's sales pitch promotes its premium membership of managers and professionals and its ability to target them in three ways: in their entirety; by business function (e.g., C-level executives, small business owners, entrepreneurs, financial professionals, IT professionals and sales professionals) and with customized lists defined by industry, job function, seniority, company size, geography, gender and number of connections. Consumer SNSs do the same. Thanks to their members' profile pages, they know not only our demographic and geographic attributes but also the books we read, movies we watch, music we enjoy and other targetable lifestyle attributes. As technology columnist Will Harris explained:

> The one thing Web 2.0 sites have in common is that they are mining information about you and

your buddies. What you like. What you like that
your buddies like. [W]hat stories you've submitted,
what demographic you're in, how other people in
your demographic react to what you post. [They]
can break users down by almost any statistic imag-
inable, then mine that data for more information
about what it is you're doing and sharing online,
and how that relates to your friends in the same or
different demographics.[16]

The SNSs are growing other revenue streams, but first and
still foremost they sell targets to advertisers.

Consumers don't object. All ad-supported media sell
our eyeballs; that's how we get free TV programs, for example. In this instance, we get a platform for self-presentation
and, so far, we insist on only one thing—control of that presentation's publicity. Not its privacy. No one creates a SNS
profile to be anonymous; we do it to be known. In this context, users want to control the scope and manner in which
our self-presentation is shared with others.

Most SNSs enable profile owners to control access to
their profiles by selecting from options on an account setting
page. The default setting on Facebook, for example, allows
only friends to access a profile. It can be reset to broaden
access to friends of friends or everyone or reset to narrow access to subsets of friends. These user-managed settings also
control access by those outside the SNS; most important, users can now decide whether search engines can spider and
retrieve their profiles. Indeed, variations around visibility
and access are one of the primary ways that SNSs differentiate themselves from each other because users are keen to
control who can see what parts of their online profiles.[17]

More dramatic, user control of profile information's publicity was *the* issue in the loud and successful protests over two
Facebook initiatives. The first was a mini-news feed that automatically pushed to a profile owner's friends any new photos,
friends, links and other changes on the profile owner's page.

The profile owner had already made that content public; she published it right on the profile page. So the issue wasn't privacy but who controls the proactive sharing of the user's profile information. Facebook's mini-feed was a usurpation, users protested and Facebook backed off. Its Beacon feature blundered in a similar way. This service pushed to the profile owners' friends her activities at other Web sites, such as movie tickets bought at Fandango, items sold on eBay and vacations planned at Travelocity. Again, users protested the unauthorized publicity and Facebook retreated.[18]

Users expressed their desire to control their publicity in a positive way, too, by demanding that their profiles and networks be portable. The argument was simple: we spend time and effort creating both and should be able to repurpose them elsewhere. The SNSs acceded. What's essential for them is to be *the* platform for their users' ongoing disclosure of personal and professional information. Since portability increases the utility of that self-disclosure for members, the SNSs are implementing it. *Facebook Connect,* for example, enables users to port and share their profile information with some 5,000 partner sites.[19]

What's essential for users is control so we can upload our better photos, announce our accomplishments, demonstrate our tastes with lists of favorites, assemble our endorsements and in other ways create whatever attractive self-presentations that we want and make them public to some or all others inside the SNS and elsewhere. Such control has made the social network profile a popular component and, for some, the anchor of their online presence.

The SNSs can't do much for one's online reputation, however. The members of one's network don't rate the profile owner's page, and they've already given their links to the profile owner in accepting the invitation to connect their pages. Without any opportunities or mechanisms for others to evaluate the profile owner, what passes for reputation on the SNSs consists of a few measures of the profile owner's activity: the profile's completeness, the frequency of updates, the inclusion of photos, the number of group memberships and other behaviors.

At the end of the day, the SNS profile is a preformatted but refreshable self-portrait presented to the profile owner's small world of strong and weak ties. It is important and popular for the control it affords for self-presentation but is in other ways limited. Presence is a single page or multiple single pages at multiple SNSs, and reputation is not available.

Blogs

Blogging is a more demanding and more powerful platform for building out one's Web presence and reputation. It's more demanding because bloggers have more freedom in how they can present themselves than profile owners do; their self-presentation is not structured by a formatted profile and not confined to a single page. Rather, bloggers present themselves by writing on topics of their choosing on their own blogs and by posting comments on others' blogs. It's more powerful because bloggers depend more on interactions with others to establish their presence than profile owners do and depend on those interactions to earn their reputations. Here's how blogs work.[20]

The word *blog* is a contraction of *Web log*, and blogging software enables users to publish diary-like entries called *posts*. Specifically, it date-stamps every post, presents the most recent first and, as posts age, automatically archives them by month. Tens of millions of people now blog regularly, and the content of all this self-publishing falls into three general categories.

Historically, the first approach to content was to share with one's readers links to little-known Web sites with brief explanations of why readers will likely find those sites interesting. All the early blogs—Steve Bogart's News, Pointers & Commentary, Dave Winer's Scripting News, Michael Sippey's The Obvious Filter and Jorn Barger's Robot Wisdom—provided this "filtering" service. This free (but not selfless) exchange of useful information is the founding ethos of the blogosphere, still delivers value and is regularly incorporated into the other two approaches to blog content, the personal and the topical.

Currently, the majority of blogs are person-centric updates. These bloggers address the question "How was your day?" with regular reports from their daily lives that range from the meaningful to the inconsequential. Typically, a personal blog is shared with the small circle of the blogger's real-life intimates. As cyber-sociologist Clay Shirky points out, most bloggers don't have audiences, they have friends.[21] SNS members behave similarly. On Facebook, for example, the average user has 120 friends but leaves comments for and chats with less than 10 of them. Similarly, the average power user has 500 friends but leaves comments for and chats with no more than 26 friends.[22] In the blogosphere and at the SNSs, personal updates are for what sociologists call the "strong ties" of each individual's "small world."

The third approach to blog content is to focus on a topic in which others are interested. Given the diversity of our interests, this can be just about anything—nature photography, windsurfing or other hobby, any business or professional competency, from polymer extrusion to estate planning, or any special situation that one shares with others, such as living with diabetes. Bloggers who aspire to punditry combine the personal and topical. Focusing on some popular topic area, such as sports, music, celebrities or politics, they use their blogs as personal op-ed columns, sharing their reactions to the current affairs of those domains.

Whatever the content, blogging is more challenging than updating a SNS profile. The SNSs offer built-in tools for users to publish personal news, upload photos, list favorites, share calendars, add third-party applications and in other ways keep their profiles interesting and fresh. All that bloggers get is the total freedom of a blank page. Fortunately, the diary-like layout calls for and the built-in functionalities support short-form content. Unfortunately, those same features also set up an expectation of regular publishing, and that requires commitment. Some editorial discipline is also needed. Bloggers must write using a consistent set of key-words so the search engines will associate those keywords with their blogs and rank those blogs high in the list of search results when those keywords are queried. Similarly, bloggers need to tag each of their posts with a consistent set of commonly used keywords so readers can search their blogs in that way. Certain courtesies are also expected, most notably, the ability to subscribe to a blog so new posts are delivered to reader's desktop or inbox.

Similarly, generating the connections within which self-presentation occurs is harder in the blogosphere than on the SNSs. On the latter, we simply invite those we already know to friend us. Person-centric bloggers also rely on family and friends. Topic-specific bloggers often start there, too, but most want to get beyond their own social systems. They do so by posting comments on others' blogs, generating content for and links back to their own. Since one or more blogs on almost every topic already exist, commenting is sometimes called joining the conversation.

Doing so takes a little work. One has to identify those blogs that address the topics to which one wants to contribute, read them regularly to identify those specific posts to which one can contribute something substantive and contribute more than occasionally to make evident the quality of one's content and the level of one's commitment. But the work involved in joining the conversation is exactly what blogging software enables, facilitates and rewards. Just as SNSs assume that the self and her network go together, blogging software assumes a blogger and her commentators go together.

This expectation of conversation is enabled by four features of all blogging software. First, at the bottom of every blog post, the software presents readers with a section in which to leave comments as well as a chronological thread of prior reader comments and the blogger's responses to those comments. Second, bloggers assign to each post a permalink, a permanent URL that enables readers and other bloggers to link directly to and discuss that particular post, regardless of its publication date. Almost as important, trackbacks is a tool that acknowledges an inbound link and returns the favor; that is, when one blog links to another, the blog receiving the link can reciprocate with a link back to the originating blog. Finally, bloggers endorse each other via a blogroll, a popular sidebar where the blogger lists and links to other bloggers whom she recommends.

By joining the conversation, a blogger can generate both content for and links to her blog. Here, as elsewhere, content builds out presence while reputation is earned when others link to that content. The more links a blog collects, the higher it will rank on a search engine's results page. As *Wired* columnist Clive Thomson explained, "The only way to influence reputation is to be part of the conversation. Being transparent, opening up, posting interesting material frequently and often is the only way to amass positive links to yourself and thus to directly influence your Googleable reputation."[23]

All this so-called link love among bloggers who are joining each other's conversations can be viewed in two opposing but equally true ways, like sides of a coin. The cynical view sees these interlinking conversational clusters as mutual admiration societies in which each blogger drives her own online reputation by patting the backs of others who will then link back to the blogger. For example, one popular blog post is a list of the best blogs on a particular topic. By posting such a "Best of…" list, the blogger not only implicitly asserts a level of expertise sufficient to filter other Web resources for other users but also attracts inbound links from the sites and bloggers who have made it onto the list. What's more, those other sites and bloggers often republish the list, generating more links to themselves and to the list-compiling blogger.[24]

Mutual interlinking for the purpose of improving one's online reputation is certainly prevalent but is too harsh as a judgment upon the blogosphere. It's human nature to like and associate with those who are similar, and all of us self-sort with others with whom we are alike. Birds of a feather do flock together, on- and offline. In fact, mapping the links among bloggers reveals that we all flock, but not in the same way. For example, a 2008 map of the links among liberal and conservative bloggers revealed a major difference. Each cluster has a core of general-interest liberal and conservative blogs and issue-specific sub-clusters, but liberals had two sub-clusters that conservatives did not: one about getting things done with Beltway politics and the other about getting things done with local activism.[25] Whatever the reasons for this difference, both blogospheres are based on preferential and reciprocal linking among those who share similar views of the world. This basic human pattern is not a flaw.

The coin's obverse presents the preferential linking patterns among bloggers as a "gift exchange," a social practice in which goods and services are given without any explicit agreement for an immediate or direct *quid pro quo*.[26] Such exchange has two results. First, it ensures that valuable resources are circulated within the community of exchangers. In the blogosphere, for example, such resources are links to URLs that others may find interesting or expertise about a topic. The amount of good content produced without pay has puzzled some, but it shouldn't. Historically, scoring the big bucks was not why we pursued art, science, religion or politics, and the same is true of our blogs, whether they are about these topics or about parenting, growing petunias or big mouth bass fishing. To be sure, our contributions in such areas do yield extrinsic rewards; they're not financial, however, but social. Specifically, what we get from others in return for freely giving to them is acknowledgement, gratitude, esteem, influence, authority and perhaps power. Offline, people who present a conference paper or sing in a church choir reap similar social rewards. It's the same online. Every gift exchange yields this second result—a social hierarchy that reflects the contributions of each to the resources being exchanged among all.

Both mutual admiration society and gift exchange are valid descriptions of the preferential linking patterns that determine the reputation of each blogger and the structure of the blogosphere. On both sides of the coin, the blogger's presence and reputation occur within and are dependent on interaction with others.

Reviews, Bookmarks and Files

Contributing bylined content to product review, social bookmarking and file-hosting sites is the narrowest path to presence and reputation. Each of these three popular Web 2.0 services is a shared repository of user-generated content. Like every informational resource, each has an internal structure—the hierarchy of classes and categories of its informational domain—within which one's self-presentation is constrained into a contribution of conforming content. Reputation is also indirect. Unlike blogger-to-blogger interlinking, reputation here is generated by rating systems in which users participate anonymously. The difference among the repositories can be described briefly before examining their similar mechanics.

Product review services collect just what the label denotes and include multi-category, category-specific and location-specific services, such as Epinions, TripAdvisor and CitySearch, respectively.[27] Major retailers' Web sites including those of Wal-mart, Target and Office Depot now also enable consumers to review products.[28] At social bookmarking sites like Digg and Delicious, the content is similar to blogging's filtering practice. Contributors share links to just-published and lesser-known URLs with the contributor's explanation of why others may find them interesting, plus multiple keyword tags of the contributor's choosing. At the file-hosting services user-generated content (UGC) consists of rich media—videos at YouTube and photos at Flickr, for example—and multiple keyword tags chosen by the contributor and by other users. The categories of YouTube's "people's choice" awards display the range of its users' contributions: Adorable, Comedy, Commentary, Creative, Inspirational, Musician of the Year and Series.

(For the record many other sites also offer UCG features.   Google Maps, for instance, enables users not only to attach reviews, photos and videos to its maps but also to make, post and share customized maps on themes users devise, from best neighborhood restaurants to children's playgrounds where the water fountains actually work. Google ranks contributors based on their reviews, maps and edits, and all contributions carry a link back to the contributors' URL. For the purpose of analysis here, however, the three repository services will be the focus.)

With all three services, establishing presence requires next to nothing—literally, a rating, a keyword, an image—although most contributors do more. All three enable users to rate the content others contributed and make that easy as well, such as asking for a rating on five-point scale or for a yes/no answer to a question about helpfulness.   New tools, like one-click favorites and in-line tag creation, are introduced regularly to the same end.[29] In addition to judgments expressed in explicit ratings, such as Top Rated and Most Favorited, many sites use the implicit judgments expressed in user behaviors, yielding such rankings as Most Viewed, Most Discussed and Most Shared.

Some services enable users to rate the raters, and the resulting reputations have consequences. At Epinions, for example, highly rated reviewers earn roles on the site—Advisor, Top Reviewer and Category Lead—each with privileges and responsibilities. The rate-the-rater system at Slashdot, a social bookmarking service for tech professionals, merits close inspection. It reveals how the organizer's values are written into the system's scoring rules and illustrates how others' drive-by judgments can be processed into credible and consequential individual reputations. Although Slashdot's system is logical, even ethical, another system may not be.

Slashdot calls itself "News for Nerds." Its contributors post short articles about tech industry news (filtering, again) and other users comment about those contributions. Slashdot's rating system ignores the contributions and focuses instead on the comments. All comments start off with a score based on the commentator's existing relationship with the Slashdot community: 0 for an anonymous user, 1 for a registered user and 2 for a registered user whose previous comments scored well. This scoring rule expresses a set of values. Anonymity is allowed but has no benefit. Registration, being knowable and accountable, is rewarded at the outset. Positive past performance doubles the starting-off score. At Slashdot, being known and being respected are legitimate basis for some users to get advantages even before the rating begins. In short, all can comment but all commentators are not equal.

Comments are then rated by moderators. Randomly selected from among registered users who have commented well and regularly over time, moderators are empowered for three days during which to choose no more than five comments to rate. Thus, the community's better commentators are empowered but cannot use that power for self-aggrandizement. In short, a lot of qualified people get a little power for a brief time.

Moderators rate comments by selecting from a drop-down list of descriptive terms: *normal, off topic, flamebait, troll, redundant, insightful, interesting, informative, funny, overrated and underrated.* Each term has a positive (+1) or a negative (-1) value that is added to the comment's starting-off score. The descriptors are, of course, arbitrary, decided upon by the service's organizers They are the arguable but not objectionable qualities upon which the organizers want to shape their community.

The moderated comment can have a resulting score that ranges from −1 to +5, and that score has consequences. Slashdot users are equipped with a threshold filter that can be set from −1, to show all comments, to +5, to show only those comments upgraded by at least three moderators. The more highly rated the comment, the more likely it is to be seen while lower rated comments may be seen by few if any at all.

Slashdot's reputation system is largely transparent, ethical and credible but also reveals three obvious perils. Using scoring rules to implement values is one. Basing scores on others' drive-by judgments is another. Using sccores to determine not only ranking but visibility itself is the third. These and probably other perils of reputation systems to come need watching. At present, fortunately, most are just popularity contests: contributors upload nuggets of content with tags and a link to their own URLs, and other users rate that content and add tags of their own.

This simplicity reflects the narrow scope these repository services afford for self-presentation and the indirect structure of interaction among their users. Unlike the SNS self-portrait and each blogger's distinctive voice, contributors to these services present themselves indirectly, through the product being reviewed, behind the lens that captured the image or one step removed from the content being tagged. As for their interactions, users contribute and rate each other's contributions independently and asynchronously of each other and use the service in the same way. In other words, online presence occurs without much self-presentation, and reputation is earned through *in*direct interaction with others. These limitations, according to some, actually encourage many users and are one source of these services' popularity.

The win-win-win is straightforward. Users get relevant content that helps them decide what to read, watch, listen to or buy, as well as whom they should trust and interact with. The repository services get incremental content at near-zero cost that directly improves user behaviors, such as longer sessions and more clicks that they can then sell to advertisers. Contributors with high scores attract traffic and links to the own URLs, links to which search engines give extra weight because they come from the repositories that are themselves well-linked. Independently contributing discrete chunks of content that are attributed, rated and linked, many users generate their online presence and reputation at these services rather than at SNSs or blogs.[30]

Presence Aggregators and People Search Engines

Of course, the more places where we leave our content, the more dispersed our cyberpersonas become. That consequence is already addressed by two meta-applications: presence aggregators and people search engines   They are "meta-" because they enable the user to gather all content *by* the user from any of the Web 2.0 platforms and narrower UGC applications as well as all content *about* the user from anywhere else on the Web and to organize those pieces of our active and passive digital footprints into coherent self-presentations at a user-managed page.

Presence aggregators, née profile aggregators, were conceived as a way for users to centralize their different SNS profiles. They're broader today and enable users to assemble in one place all their blogging, rating, reviewing, sharing and other content generated by the individual.   Some even enable users to gather their most recent activities into a news feed, called a lifestream, to which others can subscribe.[31] Like the SNSs, presence aggregators enable users to control access to their profiles, usually by account settings options, such as public, friends only or by permission. Some also enable users to create and manage their profiles in different versions and determine which version is shown to whom.[32]

The people search engines such as ClaimID, Naymz and Spoke cast a wider net in gathering up our digital fragments and take a further step: they require each registered user to authenticate that each fragment actually pertains to that user. Like all search engines they send out spiders to crawl the Web; theirs bring back all the pages that include the same proper name as the registered user. Since the same name may not refer to a single person, a problem that is called entity resolution, the people search engines present each item the spiders find to the user and ask the user to claim each item by tagging it as "about me" (passive) or "by me" (active). Most also enable users to update their pages manually, again by claiming new references as "about me" or "by me."[33]

To help ensure that their registered users are findable and found, the people search engines enable queries to be narrowed by such parameters as location, gender, and employer and by tags. Some generate tags for each person automatically by mining the content their spiders find for keywords. Others enable profile owners to attach tags of their devising. A few even enable users to rate the accuracy and relevance of a profile's tags. Finally, many people search engines will for a fee register a user's profile with the general search engines so it will appear at the top of the results list, among the other sponsored links.

Both meta-applications enable us to aggregate our cyber-pieces, organize them into one or more coherent presentations and selectively disclose them. They resemble the user-managed interfaces being designed for the virtual consumer who supplies, authenticates, updates and discloses subsets of her personally identifiable information to selected merchants. But the content and the context are different. Disclosing purchase intentions and brand preferences, we advertise ourselves as consumers to merchants. Web 2.0 invites us to promote our thoughts, tastes and activities as individuals to whoever will give us their attention. In short, one's online presence and reputation constitute a new public face for the individual.

Promoting one's personality to others through the user-managed disclosure of personal information is a novel situation. It's the antithesis of the privacy paradigm in two ways. First, the privacy paradigm assumes the individual wants her information withheld from view but, as discussed, Web 2.0 assumes the individual wants her information advanced into view. Second, the privacy paradigm assumes a passive individual. Specifically, surveys about privacy issues rarely included the individual among possible solutions and, more telling, the few that did only flummoxed the surveyors. One research group simply asserted that including the individual among the solutions "distorts the results greatly" and quickly moved on. Another team reported that consumers prefer user-controlled solutions but interpreted that to mean that consumers trust no one. Respondents to yet another survey rated consumer control higher than both business and governmental control, but the researchers ignored this finding in their discussion.[34]

The two assumptions underlying the entire Web 2.0 terrain are the opposite of the privacy paradigm: specifically, that we want to publicize ourselves and that we want to control that publicity. Both will only become more complex as new opportunities for UGC are created, more comprehensive as more of our everyday life either occurs or is replicated online and more important as one's online presence and reputation migrate from a social asset for some into a social expectation for many. The mechanics of the current services and solutions reveals that our content and our connections shape how we appear across the entire terrain, not with perfect uniformity but with enough similarity to allow generalization.

First, our content has two dimensions: presence based on the quantity of contributions and reputation based on others' judgments about the quality of those contributions. The mechanics of the different Web services shape in different ways how we build the former and earn the latter. Tomorrow's services will have their own mechanics and will likely yield presence and reputation, too. These dimensions are rooted in and express the foundational Web 2.0 assumption that users want to generate content for the attention of others. Of course, presence and reputation may not remain the only dimensions. For example, thanks to the global positioning systems on which cell phones and in-car navigation systems rely, our coordinates in real-life space and time are readily available and are well on their way to becoming socially expected.

Indeed, cyber-persona could one day have many dimensions. Today, it has two: presence and reputation.

The second feature of one's cyberpersona in the Web 2.0 world is its dependence on connections with "the other." Specifically, the profile sits at the center of its social network, the blogger is in conversation with commentators, even contributors must have peers with whom to co-create their common resource. And reputation, by definition, depends on others. This co-creation occurs in the form of links, the building blocks of any network, the Web included. Setting up a social network means inviting others to link their pages to the profile owner's page; in the blogosphere, joining the conversation means giving and receiving links to and from other bloggers; even the repository services rely on contributors' links to attribute and connect content. As network phenomena one's online presence and reputation rest on, express and emerge from one's connections—with whom one shares, to whom one links and who links back, and how often those connections are turned on by our communicating, commenting and contributing. The "machine" determines how we can appear within it, and as nodes in the linked-based network of the Web, our post-human form consists of the patterns and rhythms of our connections with other nodes.

Both content and connections—what you know and who you know—have always been important in real life, of course, but their expression in our cyber-personas may have unintended salutary consequences. Ever since modernity chunked up social life into disparate domains, modernists have worried about a self that is divided, fragmented, even multiplied. The scattered pieces of our cyber-personas confirm that situation, but the opportunity, perhaps soon the necessity of sewing those pieces together may help us give up the notion of an integrated self and become comfortable instead with a being that is plural, protean, perhaps permanently partial, even contradictory.[35] Similarly, the dependence of one's cyberpersona on its connections may help us retire, once and for all, the hero of modernism—the autonomous being whose will is exercised in choice and action—and to embrace instead a self that emerges from its interactions. Certainly, all the Web 2.0 social media examined here assume that cyber-persona is a social entity and enable its co-creation with others. Indeed, Web 2.0 assumes that not only who we are but also what we know is social, and various experiments are trying and claiming to create collective intelligence.

Notes

1 Mary Madden et al., *Digital Footprints: Online Identity Management and Search in the Age of Transparency* (Washington, DC: Pew Internet & American Life Project, 2007), www.pewInternet.org/PPF/r/229/report_display.asp. Geoff Smith of the IT consulting firm Capgemini is quoted in Paul Taylor, "Balancing the Benefits and Dangers," *Financial Times,* July 7, 1999.

2 The early history is recounted and analyzed in Howard Rheingold, *Virtual Community: Homesteading on the Electronic Frontier* (Cambridge, MA: The MIT Press, 2000).

3 Although many services enable users to make their own Web sites from page templates, the Web site as a genre is not especially author-friendly and is inhospitable to casual authors.

4 Tim O'Reilly, "What is Web 2.0?," O'Reilly, http://oreilly.com/web2/archive/what-is-web-20.html is a comprehensive and insightful overview.

5 Brands even set up their own pages on SNSs; consumers expect them to. See "Cone Finds that Americans Expect Companies to Have a Presence in Social Media," Cone, (September 25, 2008), www.coneinc.com/content1182.

6 These five Web 2.0 services were distinguishable in early 2010, but they imitate each other's successful applications and will likely become similar over time.

7 Charlene Li with Josh Bernoff, Remy Fiorentino and Sarah Glass, "Social Technographics: Mapping Participation in Activities Forms the Foundation of a Social Strategy," *Forrester Research* (April 19, 2007) offers a linear hierarchy of social media users based on the amount of their activity.

8 Pew Internet & American Life Project, *Tracking Survey, November—December,, 2006, www.pewinternet.org/~/media/Files/Questionnaire/Old/PIAL_Dec06_Tracking_FINAL_Topline.pdf.* Debra Aho Williamson, "Social Networks: Five Consumer Trends for 2009," *eMarketer* (February, 2009); "State of the Blogosphere 2008," Technorati Blog, http://blog.technorati.com/2008/09/state-of-the-blogosphere-2008.html. On a global basis, two thirds of the world's Internet population visited social networking or blogging sites, accounting for almost 10 percent of all Internet time, according to The Nielsen Company, *Global Faces and Networked Places* (2009), Nielsen Co., *Global Faces and Networked Places* (2009), http://blog.nielsen.com/nielsenwire/wp-content/uploads/2009/03/nielsen_globalfaces_mar09.pdf.

9 Atypically, younger users do not lead the adoption curve in online self-searching: 49 percent of 18—29 year olds, 54 percent of 30—49 year olds, 39 percent of 50—64 year olds and 28 percent of those ages 65 and older have searched for their names online

10 Ellen Nakashima, "Harsh Words Die Hard on the Web," *Washington Post* (March 7, 2007), www.washingtonpost.com/wp-dyn/content/article/2007/03/06/AR2007030602705_pf.html.

11 These days, individuals are encouraged to undertake personal branding in the off-line world as well and adopt traditional Madison Avenue techniques to their self-presentations in everyday life. See, for example, Peter Montoya, *The Brand Called You* (Peter

Montoya, 2002) and and Olivier Zara, "How to Create and Manage your "Personal Brand" on the Internet (Online Personal Branding)," Online Identity and Reputation, August 20, 2008, http://online-reputation.axiopole.info/2008/08/20/create-and-manage-your-personal-brand-online-personal-branding.

12 danah m. boyd, "Controlling Your Public Appearance," Apophenia (September 7, 2007, www.zephoria.org/thoughts/archives/2007/09/07/controlling_you.html.

13 danah m. boyd and Nicole B. Ellison, "Social Network Sites: Definition, History and Scholarship," *Journal of Computer-Mediated Communication 13* (2007) is an authoritative overview of social network sites. On the mapping of one's preexisting relationships into SNSs, see also Nicole B. Ellison, C. Steinfield and C. Lampe, "The Benefits of Facebook "Friends": Exploring the Relationship between College Students' Use of Online Social Networks and Social Capital," *Journal of Computer-Mediated Communication 12 (2007)* and A. Lenhart and M. Madden, "Teens, Privacy, & Online Social Networks," *Pew Internet & American Life Project Report (2007,* www.pewinternet.org/Reports/2007/Teens-Privacy-and-Online-Social-Networks.aspx.

14 David Armano, "Friendship Isn't Dead: The Strengthening of Loose Ties," Logic + Emotion, March 19, 2009, http://darmano.typepad.com/logic_emotion/2009/03/friendship-isnt-dead-the-strengthening-of-loose-ties.html.

15 On multiple SNS memberships, see Alex Patriquin, "Connecting the Social Graph: Member Overlap at OpenSocial and Facebook," Compete, November 12, 2007, http://blog.compete.com/2007/11/12/connecting-the-social-graph-member-overlap.

16 Will Harris, "Why Web 2.0 will end your privacy," Bit-techNet, June 3, 2006, www.bit-tech.net/columns/2006/06/03/Web_2_privacy/1#top (accessed February 3, 2010).

17 On users' desire for control, see Mary Madden et. al. (2007) and Samuel J. Best, Brian S. Krueger, and Jeffrey Ladewig, "Trends: Privacy in the Information Age," *Public Opinion Quarterly* vol. 70 (Fall 2006).

18 See Louise Story and Brad Stone, "Facebook Retreats on On-line Tracking," *New York Times,* November 30, 2007, www.nytimes.com/2007/11/30/technology/30face.html on the mini-feed controversy. A short summary of the Beacon controversy can be found at "Facebook Beacon," Wikipedia, http://en.wikipedia.org/wiki/Facebook_Beacon.

19 Erica Naone, "Who Owns Your Friends? Social-networking sites are fighting over control of users' personal information," *Technology Review* (July/August 2008) and Douglas Macmillan, "Facebook Connect: Your 8,000 Hidden Friends," *Business Week,* (April 2, 2009), www.businessweek.com/technology/content/apr2009/tc2009041_649562.htm.

20 Rebecca Blood, *The Weblog Handbook: Practical Advice on Creating and Maintaining Your Blog* (Cambridge, MA: Perseus, 2002) not only reviews the mechanics of blogging but also many of the important cultural assumptions and social practices of the blogosphere.

21 Clay Shirky, *Here Comes Everybody: The Power of Organizing Without Organizations* (New York: Penguin, 2008), 85—89.

22 Justin Smith, "Facebook's 'Inside Sociologist' Shares Stats on Users' Social Behavior," Inside Facebook, February 27, 2009, www.insidefacebook.com/2009/02/27/facebooks-in-house-sociologist-shares-stats-on-users-social-behavior/.

23 Clive Thomson, "The See-Through CEO," *Wired,* March 2007, www.wired.com/wired/archive/15.04/wired40_ceo.html.

24 Gary Hayes, "A Top 25 List of Social Media, Web 2.0 & Marketing 'Best-Of-Lists!" Personalize Media, www.personalizemedia. com/a-top-25-list-of-social-media-web-20-marketing-best-of-lists/

25 Julian Sanchez, "Mapping the blogosphere with spinning brain of colored dots," Ars Technica, December 21, 2008, http://arstechnica.com/old/content/2008/12/mapping-the-blogosphere-with-spinning-brain-of-colored-dots.ars

26 J. Lampel and A. Bhalla, "The Role of Status Seeking in Online Communities: Giving the Gift of Experience," *Journal of Computer-Mediated Communication,* 12(2), article 5, 2007. Bernardo A. Huberman, Daniel M. Romero and Fang Wu, "Crowdsourcing, Attention and Productivity," Social Computing Lab, HP Laboratories, Palo Alto, CA (September 12, 2008) suggests that the psychological reward of gaining the attention of others may be sufficient to explain motivation. The classic work on "gift exchange" is Marcel Mauss, *The Gift: The Form and Reason for Exchange in Archaic Societies,* originally published in French in 1925.

27 Reviewing products on blogs or third-party sites is, of course, vulnerable to payola, and some contributors do get paid or otherwise rewarded by companies about whose products they write. A handful of start-up companies even compensate bloggers on a pay-per-post basis under the euphemism "sponsored conversation." This issue is actually a molehill. Less than half (44 percent) of U.S. bloggers in 2008 made any money from their efforts, and for almost all (88 percent) the revenue source was advertising. The 11 percent who are paid to blog consists largely of corporate spokespersons, blogging journalists and middle managers at Web 2.0 companies. Meanwhile, the review sites dismiss the issue, arguing that the vastly larger number of unsponsored reviews simply drowns out the shills. Finally, the problem is intrinsically weak. A contributor's usefulness to a sponsor is based in large part on credibility and covert sponsorship ruins that. So, the universal advice to anyone writing about products is to strike whatever commercial relationships feel right and make them explicit to readers. Meanwhile, readers still

rely on the Web's root ethos, reader beware. See Anya Kamenetz, "The Perils and Promise of the Reputation Economy," *Fast Company* 131 (December 2008), www.fastcompany.com and Roger Dooley, "Anonymous Reviews Headed for Extinction," Marketing & Strategy Innovation, December 6, 2008, www.futurelab.net/blogs/ marketing-strategy-innovation/2008/12/anonymous_reviews_ headed_for_e.html.

28 At e-commerce hubs and auction sites, reputation systems generate trust between buyers and sellers who are unknown to each other; see Paul Resnick et al., *Reputation Systems: Facilitating Trust in Internet Interactions,* http://www.si.umich.edu/~presnick/papers/ cacm00/reputations.pdf. EBay's rating system is a simple +1, 0 or −1 plus comments; others use a five-point scale; still others use multiple dimensions, such as prompt response, friendliness and product quality among others.

29 Matt Rhodes, "Insight from Online Communities: Rating and Voting," Marketing and Strategy Innovation, January 28, 2009, www. futurelab.net/blogs/marketing-strategy-innovation/2009/01/ insight_from_online_communitie.html suggests that ease of use helps explain the popularity of rating and reviewing.

30 A survey of frequent contributors to product review sites found that only 25 percent engage in social networks and only 20 percent post messages to blogs; see Jack Loefhner, "Online Brand Reviewers Anxious To Help Other Buyers," MediaPost, December 18, 2007, www.mediapost.com/publications/?fa=Articles.showArticle&art_ aid=72841.

31 For a critique, see Josh Catone, "The Lifestreaming Backlash," ReadWriteWeb, (March 24, 2008) www.readwriteWeb.com/archives/the_lifestreaming_backlash.php.

32 Stan Schroeder, "20 Ways To Aggregate Your Social Networking Profiles," Mashable, July 17, 2007, http://mashable.

com/2007/07/17/social-network-aggregators/ reviews profile centralizers.

33 See Erica Naone, "Searching for Humans," *Technology Review*, August 20, 2007, www.technologyreview.com/communications/19270/; Paula J. Hane, "People Search Tools Populate the Web," *Information Today*, September 1, 2007, http://newsbreaks.infotoday.com/nbReader. asp?ArticleId=37403; Michael Arrington, "Spock's New People Engine," *TechCrunch*, April 11, 2007, www.techcrunch.com/2007/04/11/exclusive-screenshots-spocks-new-people-engine/.

34 See Michael A. Turner and Robin Varghese, *Making Sense of the Privacy Debate: A Comparative Analysis of Leading Consumer Privacy Studies* (New York: The Direct Marketing Association, 2001). The absence of control is likely one factor in consumers' "visceral reactions" to privacy that precede any balancing of benefits and risks, an observation reported by Fred H. Cate and Richard J. Varn, *The Public Record: Information Privacy and Access* (Des Moines, Iowa: Coalition for Sensible Public Records, 1999).

35 Those who argue along this line include Kenneth Gergen, *The Saturated Self: Dilemmas of Identity in Contemporary Life* (New York: Basic Books, 1991); Donna Harraway, *Simians, Cyborgs, Women: The Reinvention of Nature* (New York: Routledge, 1991), 144—181; Robert Jay Lifton, *The Protean Self: Human: Resilience in the Age of Fragmentation* (New York: Basic Books, 1993); Emily Martin, *Flexible Bodies: Tracking Immunity in American Culture from the Days of Polio to the Age of AIDS* (Boston: Beacon Press, 1994); Sherry Turkle, *Life on the Screen: Identity in the Age of the Internet* (New York: Simon & Schuster, 1995), 180 and 256; Poster (2001), 37 and 75 and Hayles, 26—32.

CHAPTER 6

THINKING TOGETHER

Our ready-made individuality, our identity is no
more than an accidental cohesion in the flux of time.
— D. H. Lawrence, "The Crown" (1915)

The network knows what the nodes don't.
— Kim Rachmeier, Internet advisor and investor (2008)

The mission of all computing is to augment human intelligence, and the Internet holds out a particular potential in this regard. It enables many users to connect with many other users and is unlike other communications media. The telephone network connects one person with one other person; it's a *one-to-one* medium. The Internet does that, too, with e-mail and telephony. TV, radio, magazines and newspapers are *one-to-many* media; they enable one "person," the broadcaster or publisher, to connect with many persons—viewers, listeners and readers. Web sites and blogs also enable the one to connect with the many. Alone among media the Internet enables *many-to-many* communication and holds out the prospect that we can learn how to think better together.

This has already brought power to the people. Even before the Web came along, the Internet was famous for enabling people to find each other and create conversational communities on bulletin board systems, in chat rooms, in discussion forums, even via the e-mail lists known as LISTSERVs.[1]

Today, with the advent of Web 2.0 applications, which enable users to generate and share content, forming groups in the grassroots has become easy, quick and cheap. One result is a proliferation of groups that have narrow social value, low commercial value or both. Economically impossible under the old cost structure of communications, such groups flourish now that communications power is in the hands of the people.[2]

A grander understanding of this empowerment sees the surface of our planet wrapped in a cloak of trunk lines, radio waves and electronic circuits, humming with the communication of humankind, and proposes that something positive will emerge. The humanistic version anticipates a future in which meaning will emerge from an evolutionary ebb and flow of discourse within parameters and a discourse-based process of always-provisional outputs will augment not merely our intelligence but more profoundly our humanity.[3] The post-humanist version foresees the emergence of a super-organism—a networked intelligence, sensate, self-governing and capable of learning—displaying what *Wired* editor Kevin Kelly calls "intelligence without reason."[4] Both humanist and post-humanist visions center on the concept of emergence, and to understand the promise of many-to-many connectivity requires that term be defined.

Emergence occurs when the interactions of simple entities, acting locally and autonomously, turn into complex entities that act globally and holistically. In the natural world, the flocking of birds and the schooling of fish are examples of how many simple entities become one complex entity. The flock and the school emerge from the behaviors of birds and fish, but the complex entities have capabilities and functions of their own, greater than and different from what individual birds and fish have. Bees and ants are even more impressive. They build hives and colonies that have permanence but they don't have master plans. Those complex entities emerge from the interactions of bees and ants acting locally and autonomously; the emergent hives and colonies function and respond globally as wholes in ways the bees and ants cannot. In short, emergence occurs when a whole emerges from but is different from the sum of the parts.

The World Wide Web also displays emergent properties. There's no master plan here either, but the Web does take on a shape that emerges from the links its users insert to connect one node to another. According to Internet impresario Tim O'Reilly:

> Hyperlinking is the foundation of the web. As users add new content, and new sites, it is bound in to the structure of the web by other users discovering the content and linking to it. Much as synapses form in the brain, with associations becoming stronger through repetition or intensity, the web of connections grows organically as an output of the collective activity of all web users.[5]

This ongoing activity is self-reinforcing. Some nodes get more inbound links than others do. Those better-linked nodes are more findable, attracting more visits, from which those nodes will get even more inbound links. The search engines reflect these decisions. They count the number of inbound links as a measure of a node's "authority" and rank nodes with more links higher in their lists of results. And they reinforce these decisions: the higher ranked nodes get even more visits, even more inbound links and even higher ranks in the search results. Some people disparage this bottom-up "authority" structure and suggest it's better defined as "popularity according to the Web's most prolific linkers." Judgments aside, a functional and responsive global order emerges within the Web from the independent linking of its autonomous users.[6]

In other words, cyberspace seems a particularly hospitable context for attempts to generate wisdom from crowds. In a network where each autonomous entity can connect to every other and where many-to-many connections can be enabled quickly, easily and at near-zero cost, it's only logical to ask: can we configure modes of interaction among these nodes so that the outputs of their interactions are greater than and different from the sum of their inputs? The three applications examined here take on a modest version of this quest. Specifically, crowdsourcing, recommender systems and prediction markets enable the many to produce and share content. As always, the specific mechanics of each application determines whether our thinking together produces intelligence, groupthink or something else. Before addressing those specifics, however, certain common features can and should be delineated.

In general, collective intelligence can be defined as a process in which many "agents" work, each in their own time and at their own pace, on parts of a larger project without a plan or supervision and produce knowledge. The common attributes are:

Purpose	The output of the collective endeavor is specific and understood.
Divisibility	The output is divisible such that agents can produce inputs toward its completion.
Parallelism	Agents work autonomously and concurrently.
Equality	Agents start off with the same privileges and responsibilities.
Hierarchy	In some configurations, agents can earn more privileges and responsibilities.
Transparency	The machinery of decision making and its use are visible.
Diversity	Difference in the agents' skills, expertise or perspectives is required if the output requires balance, innovation or reliability.
Systemic Effect	The output is attributable to the system that connects the agents at a higher level than the agents themselves and is not

achievable by individual agents even with infinite resources.

The last attribute is the difference between aggregating individual intelligences and catalyzing collective intelligence. The following analysis suggests where this does and does not occur.

Crowdsourcing

Crowdsourcing refers to the use of Web 2.0 applications to enable a large group of people outside an organization to contribute to the completion of a work task. It's not a new production model. The *Oxford English Dictionary* was compiled that way back in the 19th century. What's new are the scale and low cost of online connectivity, and three types of crowdsourcing can already be distinguished: worksourcing, ideasourcing and expertsourcing.

Worksourcing involves tapping a crowd of people to complete repetitive tasks that require human intelligence; otherwise some machine would be performing the tasks. Two volunteer projects, for example, leverage the fact that humans are better than machines at pattern recognition. Four research universities set up Galaxy Zoo, a Web site where volunteers are classifying over a million galaxies as elliptical or spiral and by the directions of their spin. Similarly, Stardust@Home, hosted by The Planetary Society, invites volunteers to find interstellar dust particles from among some 700,000 3-D images of the Stardust spacecraft's collector plate.[7] Not to be outdone, the social sciences are trying to access what's called local or situational knowledge—information specific to a time and place. The Library of Congress recently posted thousands of its photographs to photo-hosting site Flickr and asked the public to answer: *What is this? Who is this? When was it taken?* The National Archives launched a similar project with online versions of its documents.

In the for-profit sector, Amazon.com has a worksourcing initiative called the Mechanical Turk, honoring the

18th century chess-playing automaton. It pays a few pennies for trivial tasks that only human can do, like identifying performers on music CDs and choosing appropriate categories for certain products. Not all worksourcing tasks are so trivial, however, and the potential consequences of worksourcing in the marketplace are not entirely benign.

Some worksourcing sites operate reverse auctions in which freelancers compete for projects by underbidding each other. Such bid-for-work markets have been set up in such categories as graphic design and copywriting, sales and marketing, financial and managerial services and computer programming. A few sites offer "on spec" assignments, which means doing the work without any guarantee of payment just to win the assignment and, if selected, get paid. The "winner" gets a nominal fee, all the others get zip and the company gets the work at a fraction of what a service firm might charge. The logical endpoint has already been reached. IStockphoto.com quickly became the third-largest seller in the $2 billion stock photography business by selling images at rock-bottom prices; it can do so because more than 90 percent of its photographers are amateurs who sign away their royalty rights. At the end of the day, piecework, whether by volunteers on science projects or low-bidding online freelancers, is neither collective nor intelligent.

A second type of crowdsourcing is ideasourcing, organized at an "ideagora"—a Web site where companies post problems, users propose solutions and the one who solves the problem wins a prize. Despite the fancy labels, the structure is an inducement prize contest and also quite old. The most famous of such contests is the Longitude Prize, announced by the British government in 1714; the most famous winner of such a contest is aviator Charles Lindberg, who claimed the Orteig Prize in 1927 for the first solo flight across the Atlantic. The structure still works. The Ansara X Prize, $10 million for the first nongovernmental organization to launch a reusable manned spacecraft into space twice within two weeks, was awarded in 2004. In 2009, a team of mathematicians won a $1 million prize from DVD rental company Netflix for improving its recommender system by 10 percent. In another recent contest, Canadian mining company Goldcorp made available online some 400 megabytes of geological data about its Ontario property and offered $575,000 to anyone whose data analysis could pinpoint where gold could be found. A small consultancy in Australia won. So did Goldcorp: it collected from all contest entries 110 targets, of which over 80 percent proved productive, yielding 8 million ounces of gold worth more than $3 billion.

What's new about ideagoras is not the inducement prize contest but the cost efficiency of offering multiple smaller challenges and, more important, the ability to engage diverse perspectives on the same problem. At InnoCentive.com, an ideagora spun off from drug company Eli Lilly, *seekers* such as Boeing, Dow, DuPont and Novartis post specific technical problems, or *challenges*. The site's *solvers* are more than 100,000 scientists from 175 countries, in such fields as chemistry, biochemistry, biology and material sciences. Their solutions have included a compound for skin tanning, a method for preventing snack chip breakage, a mini-extruder design for brick making and many others. InnoCentive collects a fee from the seeker for posting its challenge and, if solved, a finder's fee, roughly 40 percent of the cash prize, usually between $10,000 and $25,000.

InnoCentive's high solve rate is due largely to the fact that the solvers come from a very broad range of disciplines, far more diverse than the disciplines inside the seeker company. For example, Colgate-Palmolive's internal R&D team, unable to find a more efficient way to fill toothpaste tubes, posted that challenge. An electrical engineer won; he proposed putting a positive charge on fluoride powder and then grounding the tube, collecting $25,000 for a few hours work. As Harvard Business School professor Karim R. Lahkani, who studied InnoCentive, explained, "The further the problem was from the solver's expertise, the more likely they were to solve it," often by applying specialized knowledge or

instruments developed for other purposes.[8] This leverages
a well-known aspect of human intelligence: applying the
perspective of one discipline to a problem in another always
sparks previously unasked questions and, sometimes, good
answers.[9] The inducement prize contest, whether offering
one challenge or many, online or offline, does not generate collective intelligence, however. On the contrary, it's designed to attract the uniquely qualified mind to step forward
out from the crowd.

A third type of crowdsourcing, expertsourcing, aims to
harvest subject matter expertise. Commercial sites like Yahoo Answers, Ask Metafilter, AllExperts (née Expert Central)
and Windows Live QnA (beta) enable users to ask and answer questions but are small successes at best. The shining
example is the nonprofit Wikipedia, the online encyclopedia created by an all-volunteer army of contributors. They
build it using a collaborative authoring application called a
wiki. This software enables multiple users to make edits to
the same text, to store and access all versions with all changes
and to restore a previous version. On Wikipedia anyone can
access these capabilities, that is, anyone can initiate and write
an article and can add to, edit, rewrite entirely or restore articles without supervision or approval.

Wikipedia's growth has been explosive. From 31 articles
in January 2001, it amassed more than 17,000 within the first
12 months and today has more than 3 million articles in English and 14 million articles in more than 260 languages. It's
free and popular; in 2009 it was the 5th most visited site on
the Web. As for quality, it's spotty but still impressive, given
how the content is sourced. A comparison with Encyclopedia Britannica conducted by *Nature* magazine found 162 fac-
tual errors, omissions or misleading statements in Wikipedia
and 123 in the Britannica. The magazine concluded that
Wikipedia came close in terms of accuracy, to which the Britannica folks retorted that 30 percent more accurate was not
insignificant. In theory, Wikipedians will fix these flaws in
the normal course of using the site; indeed, they fixed all the

errors *Nature* found within just a few days. It's also dispirit-
ing but not surprising that the entry for TV's cartoon series
The Flintstones is twice as long as that for Thomas Jefferson.
Time will tell how the site's content evolves, but an examination of its social production—the how of its user-generated
content—suggests that Wikipedia is doing pretty much everything right.

The purpose is specific. It's not task- or problem-specific
like worksourcing or ideasourcing; rather, there's a normative
consensus about the output. All contributors are on the same
page about what an encyclopedia entry *should* contain: one
or more definitions of the topic, some historical account of
origins and development, some assessment of best-known impacts in one or more domains and, if there's controversy, sum-
maries of the different positions and their chief advocates.

If an article looks anything like that, others can improve
it. A contributor can correct spelling, fix punctuation, add
a citation, rewrite a sentence, flesh out a paragraph or write
an entire article. The output is divisible and the inputs are
scalable.

All contributors start off equal, but as in all volunteer
endeavors, some do more than others. Indeed, the project's
success has come to rely on a self-selecting cadre of highly active users who contribute more articles of their own, who edit
more articles of others and who adopt and tend to a set of
pages, eliminating vandalism and deciding on corrections.

Diversity can be discerned as an article evolves through
successive iterations, but it's manifest in the pages behind
each article. That's where contributors discuss and sometimes argue the merits of proposed changes to content.
What's visible on the article's main page is the content on
which they agree, at least at the moment.

When diversity turns into disputes, Wikipedia has a for-
mal and complex system for collective adjudication of these
matters that's transparent to all. If that doesn't work, the
site's administrators can step in with a decision. They have
even shut down public editing of articles on a handful of

topics, such as the Iraq War and abortion, because they are so often vandalized by zealots.

Whether Wikipedia has a systemic effect is arguable. Wiki software enables multiple users to write and revise the same content, but largely because it enables each user to contribute independently of the others. The software doesn't connect contributors one to another in any novel way, and successive versioning, while yielding improvement over time, is not greater than or different from the sum of its inputs. Rather, multi-authored versioned content *is* the sum of its inputs, and in theory individual agents with infinite resources could produce equivalent output.[10]

Rather, Wikipedia's innovation is a set of attitudes about knowledge, specifically, that it should be always provisional and universally open. There is no last word. No one has final say. Of course, the creation of knowledge has always been an ongoing social process, and knowledge always a social output. Whether Wikipedia's decision to hold knowledge permanently open to everyone changes anything is yet to be determined.

Ratings, Rankings and Recommendations

Rating, ranking and filtering systems are all over the Web, and all have the same goal: to aid in selecting items from a set of items by distinguishing some items from others. Among these systems two types generate collective intelligence—a new type of higher-order content that is different from the sum of the inputs, that is useful and reliable and that can be produced in no other way. The particulars of these accomplishments are most easily understood in the context of the different benefits that each system delivers.

Rating systems invite users to score the items of a set, whether the system is offline, like Zagat's restaurant guides or, online, such as those offered at Amazon, Netflix and Trip Advisor,   As aids to decision making, they have two weaknesses. First, the raters rate each item independently of, not relative to, others. So, two similar items, such as a French cookbook by Julia Child and another by Jacques Pépin, could get the same score. Indeed, two dissimilar items, such as a French cookbook and a diet cookbook, could also get the same score. In short, items scored in isolation don't necessarily distinguish one item from another.

Second, the distributions of item scores can also be hard to make useful for decision making. The illustration shows four distributions of ratings, using a five-point scale, with 1 being the lowest score and 5 being the highest. The pattern of each is easy to discern, but only two are easy to put to use. Distribution 1 shows that a lot of raters like the item and would encourage a user to select it. Distribution 2 shows that a lot of raters dislike the item and would discourage a user from selecting it. Distribution 3 is also easy to interpret—raters are polarized about the item; they either love it or hate it—but that isn't especially helpful to a user in deciding whether or not to select it. Similarly, Distribution 4 looks like the normal bell curve, which doesn't help much in deciding about the item, either. In short, rating systems, whether they display scores or distributions of scores, consider each item in isolation and offer little help in making a decision to select this item rather than that item.

Frequency Distributions
5-point rating scale

| | Many Like | Many Dislike | Either/ Or | Normal Bell Curve |

Measuring items relative to each other is the job of ranking systems, of which the biggest and best known by far is

Google. All search engines do this job. They enable a user to enter a word or phrase into a dialogue box, submit that to the engine and get back a list of Web pages related to that word or phrase. The challenge for the engines is not finding Web pages that are relevant to the word or phrase but figuring out an order in which to present those pages. That means ranking each relevant Web page relative to every other relevant Web page on the strengths of its correlations with the word or phrase that's being searched.

Google's founding innovation was a way to rank Web pages relative to each other that was unique to and meaningful on the Web. The PageRank algorithm, named for Google cofounder Larry Page, counts a link from one Web page to another as a "preferential attachment," as an implicit endorsement from the source page and a unit of authority for the target page. Web pages with more inbound links have more authority and get ranked higher than other pages in the list of results the engine presents to the user. This rank order is self-reinforcing. In the offline world, the rich get richer. In the online world, the higher ranked Web pages get more visits and from that more links, so the well-linked pages get even more well-linked.

Of course, search engines do more than count inbound links to determine the order of the Web pages they present. They apply text-mining to the content of each Web page to identify its keywords, scan and integrate the metatags (more keywords) attached to each Web page and factor in which links get clicked for different search terms, among many other techniques. The goal is to measure the relevance of each Web page to the search term and thereby rank the relevant Web pages into an order.

Although relative ranking is more helpful than isolated ratings, neither system can tell the user which item is better for the user. The results of both are nonspecific, applying to everyone in general and no one in particular, and there's validity in the criticism of both ratings and rankings as popularity contests. Tech Memorandum, for example, is a Web site that aggregates the headlines of technology-related news stories. Like the search engines, it determines the order in which to present these headlines by tracking what links people click, what links they insert and so on. It then processes those choices to determine which headlines to show in what order on its home page. The home page changes every five minutes as the site processes new data. The result of this link-based popularity contest is predictable: the home page tends to publish what its readers already know.

While ratings and rankings systems present nonspecific results intended for everyone, recommender systems present results that suit the individual user. They proactively put in front of the user those items from the set that have not yet been seen by the user but in which the user is likely to be interested.[11] While search engines help *all* users *find* items they're looking for, recommender systems help *individual* users *discover* items they don't yet know about, would not likely have found on their own and will probably like. In short, recommender systems generate "relevant discovery."

There are two types of recommender systems. A content-based system recommends items to the user that are similar to items the user preferred or selected in the past. It has no collective dimension and is ignored here. A recommender system based on collaborative filtering puts items in front of the user that other users with similar tastes preferred or selected in the past. This approach is collective; it harvests inputs from the many—some, but not all, others—to predict the utility of an item to an individual user.

Amazon.com's "Customers Who Bought This Item Also Bought" function is the best-known collaborative filter, but many sites offering cultural products, such as Netflix (movies) and LastFM (music), use this approach because the number and variety of items and the users' preferences regarding them are vast.[12] Anyone who's used any of these sites more than a few times knows that relevant discovery is a genuine informational benefit. As a system that meets all the criteria for collective intelligence, it deserves a close look.

Collaborative filtering can be active or passive, depending on how user inputs are collected. Active collaborative filtering solicits and collects *expressed* inputs. It asks a user to *rate* an item on a sliding scale, *rank* a set of items from most favorite to least favorite or *list* those items he likes. The big advantage is that the collected data express actual cognitive activity; in short, the score is an actual assessment. The big downsides are that the data is limited to scores on items and that one can collect only so much expressed data before respondent fatigue sets in.[13]

Passive collaborative filtering solves both of those problems by gathering *behavioral* data. Instead of collecting a score for an item, these systems collect data on a broad range of item-specific user behaviors—what items a user views, saves, downloads, prints, shares, tags, comments on, links to and buys. Second, passive systems collect data from almost everyone. Typically, their default setting for data collection is opt-in; unless users actively opt out, their behaviors are recorded and put in the pool.

Most users do not opt out. Click-throughs are the currency of recommender systems. By allowing the site to capture and compare preference-revealing clicks, each user improves his own filter, and everyone else's, and gets increasingly better recommendations in the ordinary course of using the site. Moreover, there's a network effect: the more people who use the system, the better it gets. As the breadth and depth of the data increase, the predicted utility of a specific item to a specific user comes closer to the actual utility of that item to that user. In plain English, more recommendations (predicted items) become sales. That's why Netflix offered $1 million as an inducement to anyone who could improve its recommender system by 10 percent. Accurate recommendations drive sales because they deliver value—unknown but relevant items—to the user.

Of course, passive collaborative filtering is not perfect. Because filtering requires there be a flow to filter, two pump-priming problems can occur but typically don't last long. The "first rater" problem refers to a new *item,* which has not yet received any ratings from any users, cannot be correlated with rated items and is therefore never recommended. The "cold start" problem refers to a new *user* who has not yet rated any items, cannot be correlated with other users who have rated items and therefore never receives personalized recommendations. There's also a challenge in interpreting behaviors, such as items viewed, downloaded, shared and so forth as evaluations. Most sites are careful and sophisticated in making such imputations. Some enable users to rate the items the system recommends, thereby adding expressed judgments (active filtering) to behavioral data (passive filtering). Amazon, for example, invites users to fix each recommendation by selecting "I own it" or "Not interested" as well as to fix the prior behavior that prompted the recommendation by selecting "This was a gift" or "Don't Use for Recommendations." Amazon then removes these items from the user's filter, improving the accuracy of its recommendations.

Among the rating, ranking and recommender systems, collaborative filtering meets the criteria of collective intelligence. Its machinery processes inputs from the many—some but not all others—into discoveries for the one, and relevant discovery—items previously unknown but likely to interest the user—is substantively new knowledge that could not be created in other ways. It just needs pointing out that, as with other Web 2.0 applications, getting value from collaborative filtering requires a willingness to be visible to the machine. Our transparency provides the fuel from which the machine generates value.

Prediction Markets

If Big Brother had a little brother, he'd be retired U.S. Navy Vice Admiral John M. Poindexter. In the wake of the 9/11 terrorist attacks, Poindexter was appointed director of the Information Awareness Office (IAO), the data-mining unit of the Pentagon's R&D unit, the Defense Advanced

Research Projects Agency (DARPA). His first proposal, the Total Information Awareness plan, would have had the federal government scouring the country's databases for every consumer's credit card purchases, car rentals, library books, airline ticket purchases, hotel stays, telephone bills and the like, ultimately in real time, looking for patterns that might indicate terrorist planning or activity. The idea got nixed on privacy grounds.

His next idea was an online market in terrorism futures, and it cost him his job. Named the Policy Analysis Market (PAM), this e-market would have enabled traders to bet and win money by correctly predicting future terrorist-related events in the Middle East, such as assassinations, coups d'etat, bombings and missile attacks. Traders would express their predictions about such events by buying and selling futures contracts, just like commodities traders buy and sell contracts on pork bellies, coffee and other futures. Those who thought a politician would be assassinated or a government toppled by a certain date would buy the contract on that future and, if the event occurred before that date, would make money. Those who thought the murder or coup would not occur would sell the contract and, if the event did not occur, would make money. The Economist Intelligence Unit and Net Exchange, a company that makes software for trading financial derivatives, helped design the nuts and bolts.

Politicians elbowed their way to the nearest bully pulpit and editorial writers sharpened their pencils to denounce PAM as "grotesque," "ridiculous," "morally wrong," "bizarre," "ghoulish" and a "macabre bazaar of death and destruction." Some media, including both the liberal *New York Times* (July 31, 2003) and the conservative *Wall Street Journal* (August 1, 2003), defended PAM, but the outrage was too great. The market never launched and Poindexter resigned soon thereafter.[14]

This public relations disaster was unfortunate because prediction markets have an excellent track record. The oldest is the Iowa Electronic Markets. Organized by the

University of Iowa under special clearance from the Commodity Futures Trading Commission and operating continuously since 1988, these public markets have consistently proven more accurate than all traditional polling methods in not only predicting but also approximating the outcomes of U.S. and foreign elections, primaries and other political events. The Hollywood Stock Exchange, a prediction marketplace for movie fans, does equally well at both. It not only outperforms the studios' traditional methods for forecasting opening weekend box office receipts but also comes uncannily close to the actual receipts. This market does just as well in predicting the Oscar awards, not just the winners but the 40 individuals the industry selects as nominees across eight different categories. In short, these markets can not only predict but also approximate outcomes that are close to observed realities.

The U.S. business community is actively exploring the potential uses of this predictive machinery. According to various news reports, conference papers and prediction market software vendors, prediction markets are or have been used at Abbott Labs, Arcelor Mittal, Best Buy, Corning, Edmunds, Eli Lilly, General Electric, Google, Hewlett-Packard, Intel, Masterfoods, Microsoft, Motorola, Qualcomm, Pfizer, Renault, Siemens and Starwood Hotels. Their interest and activity is driven by two factors: one general, the other specific.

The general driver is a shift in the practice of knowledge management. Traditionally, knowledge managers focused on archiving, protecting and accessing their companies' patents, trademarks, business plans, research, customer lists and other intellectual property. But there's another type of business knowledge—the know-how in employees' heads that emerges from, exists within and evolves among interacting employees trying to get the day's work done—and knowledge management today tries to capture this *situated* cognition. Askme. com, for example, uses a version of expertsourcing to enable companies to locate knowledge within their organizations, but most companies rely on "social network analysis." This practice involves surveilling and mapping day-to-day contacts among employees to identify who talks with whom, when and about what; who has expertise, who has influence and who has connections and who depends on whom to solve which problems in order to identify and locate existing situated cognition.[15] Prediction markets for employees also tap situated cognition, but the purpose is to generate new and higher order intelligence.

That's the specific driver behind businesses experimenting with prediction markets; they deliver reliable intelligence that businesses need. Internal markets for sales forecasting have been widely implemented with great success. Anonymous employees playing for nominal prizes have proved consistently more accurate than surveys of both salespersons and customers for predicting sales. In absolute terms, the prediction markets' results come close to marketplace's actual results. Sales forecasting involves a simple outcome, predicting more or less of a single continuous variable with historical data available to traders, and some companies are exploring whether similar predictive accuracy can be achieved for other types of outcomes.[16]

The results have not been disclosed but here's what's been tried. A top-10 pharmaceutical company has deployed markets to predict the dispositions of regulatory issues, the relative performance of same-category drugs in treating illnesses, changes in drug prices and healthcare benefits, the relative probabilities of different R&D projects coming in on time and on budget and the number of New Molecular Entities that will be approved by the Food and Drug Administration. Since 2008, Google has set up internal markets that offered contracts on some 275 outcomes on sales and other company performance variables, as well as on such external events as mergers and acquisitions. General Electric has used prediction markets to generate new business ideas; Starwood Hotels, to select marketing campaigns.[17] Start-up company

Inkling Markets enables a company's employees to generate probabilities on business risks, while MIT's Sloan School of Business has set up markets for trading product attributes in such categories as automobiles and computers and service features in such categories as ski resorts and hotels. These markets stabilize quickly, often in less than 20 minutes, revealing the relative value of competing sets of product attributes or service features.[18]   Using older methods, that task would take a lot of money and many months to complete.

Prediction markets will not, of course, displace business' traditional methods, but any organization that can frame its informational needs as predictions can set up markets where the trading patterns of experts, frontline personnel or customers will generate reliable probabilities on outcomes. Such markets are especially useful in situations where information or knowledge is distributed among many, is hard to gather or is difficult to verbalize, where new information flows in continuously and updates are required and where there's little relevant or reliable historical data about the outcome. Such conditions are widespread across the business landscape and since the Internet makes setting up such markets easy, quick and inexpensive, these markets are likely to become even more widespread. They transform the incomplete information and diverse judgments of individuals about the probabilities of future events into collective assessments that accurately correlate with actuality.

How the public might benefit from such prediction machinery is not clear, and other than the university-based Iowa Electronic Markets, there are only three prediction markets in which ordinary folks can participate. As mentioned earlier, the Hollywood Stock Exchange enables movie fans to trade stocks and bonds in movie stars and movies. The owner, financial services firm Cantor Fitzgerald, uses the data in servicing its entertainment industry clients. The MIT magazine *Technology Review* hosts markets in which readers predict such tech industry milestones as the price per kilowatt/hour

of solar energy and the percentage of U.S. households using the Internet for telephone service. The purpose is to
demonstrate to advertisers that its readers are leading edge.
Consensus Point, a company that designs and hosts prediction
markets for private clients, operates the Foresight Exchange.
This public site offers markets on such outcomes as the year-
end price of gasoline, a major earthquake occurring on the
U.S. West Coast and the end of celibacy for Roman Catholic
priests; marketing is the purpose here as well, specifically to
showcase the company's software. Various public sites enable users to make predictions on a wide variety of events in
popular culture, such as sports competitions, awards shows
and celebrity shenanigans, hoping to attract and sell eyeballs
to advertisers. But they are not markets. Participants do not
interact. They predict independently and the sites tally their
predictions like a survey—this percentage predicts this outcome, that percentage predicts the other.

In contrast, markets are based on the interaction among
participants, an interaction that turns divergent individual
judgments about an outcome into a single assessment on
which all agree, a price. The outcome they are predicting is
always "fuzzy," meaning it has multiple causal variables that
are only partially known, such as a company's future profits.
The individuals have always incomplete, sometimes biased,
always rational but nonetheless subjective judgments about
the fuzzy outcome. Trading is their conversation. To trade,
each must self-quantify his judgment about that outcome
relative to the trading price, a combination of all others'
similarly self-quantified judgments. Through trading, the diversity of individual judgments is unified into a higher order
assessment upon which all agree: the trading price is *their*
consensus from one moment to the next. In general, humans excel at solving ill-defined problems—those that have
complex goals, multiple solutions, or a changing nature—
through the application of knowledge and experience. Markets transform what each of us can do into something many
of us can do even better together.

Futures markets in particular are organized so that the trading price reflects the current consensus about whether a specific outcome will occur on a settlement date. For example, sales of Product A will reach X units by the end of the month.[19] Traders buy and sell contracts on the outcome. The contract's price always starts at 50. Its final price is always either 100 if the outcome occurs or 0 if it does not. In between it varies. If traders think the outcome is increasingly likely to occur, the price goes up; if they think the outcome is decreasingly likely, the price goes down. At any moment the price expresses traders' collective consensus on the outcome's probability. If the contract "sales of Product A will reach X units" is trading at 38, the crowd at that time thinks there's a 38 percent chance that outcome will occur.[20]

Prediction markets can go disastrously wrong in myriad ways and have to be set up just right to generate reliable probabilities. One element that's essential is diversity among market participants.[21] Diversity is the raw material; the market creates value by synthesizing diversity into a higher order intelligence on which all agree: the probability of the outcome according to them all. That's why DARPA's market in terrorism futures intended to invite not only government intelligence analysts but also academics, business executives, journalists, economists and other experts. Expertise ensured that the information of each would be relevant and, because it was narrowly specialized, diverse by definition. For the same reason, when companies set up internal markets for sales forecasting, they typically restrict participation to salespeople but make sure to include old hands and new hires who are working different types of trade zones, geographic territories and target markets. Anonymity is usually added as well to escape organizational politics, peer influences and personal careerism that can impinge upon being honest with oneself in assessing outcomes and in openly expressing assessments that may be different from others.

What's new about prediction markets is not the mechanism. For most of the 20th century, commodities exchanges have offered contracts on futures.[22] Rather, the innovation is a small but transformative change: the prediction markets invert the relationship between money and information. In financial markets, the purpose of trading is to make money; the trading price is an informational byproduct. In prediction markets, making money is not the purpose. On the contrary, the amount of money one can win for correct predictions is always limited to nominal amounts, just enough to ensure the quality of the trading price. That is, having a stake in being right motivates traders to ignore what they may want to occur (preferences) and focus on what they think actually will occur (probabilities).[23] In prediction markets, money is a means; the end is accurate probabilities from the crowd.

Because the Internet enables many-to-many connectivity, its potential for creating collective intelligence is among its most important promises. Although many applications claim to do so, they don't hold up to scrutiny. Using the crowd as a pool of individual intelligences has nothing collective about it, no matter if it's volunteers picking out space dust, freelancers underbidding each other for project work or scientists solving technical problems for prizes. To be sure, these applications have benefits, but they don't create collective intelligence. The Web's rating and ranking systems count up individual-level data, the expressed preferences of scores and the preferential attachments of links, but like their offline analogs, these aggregations don't emerge from any systemic effect in the interaction among raters or linkers. Finally, among the filter-based recommender systems, the content-based method is based solely on the prior behavior of the individual and doesn't qualify.

Three applications do qualify. The first, expertsourcing, is borderline, however. Successive editing of the same text does yield improvement, but each iteration is the work of an individual. The accretive result is better than the sum of its inputs but not by much, and it's not different in kind from its inputs. Collaborative filters and predictive markets qualify because they connect their agents in ways that generate knowledge at a level higher than their agents' aggregated inputs. The former connects us analytically through algorithms that transform the behaviors of many into recommendations for one. The latter connect us as traders, and our trading transforms our many divergent judgments into unified consensual assessments.

Even claims that relevant discovery and reliable probabilities are collective intelligence must be carefully expressed. Their mechanisms are not new. The algorithms of collaborative filtering are advanced versions of the predictive modeling practiced by data-based marketing, operating in near real time on a lot more and a lot better data. As for futures markets, they first became famous in 1636 when Tulip mania swept over Holland, England and France. Using the Internet makes implementation faster, better and cheaper but not different.

Rather, what's new is a set of attitudes about knowledge that are applied to implementation. The innovation at Wikipedia is not sequential editing or the wiki software but the decisions that all articles will be held open and open to all. The always-provisional text and universal access articulate without words the views that there is no last word and no final authority on any topic. The innovation in collaborative filters is not the mathematics but the decision to treat all items as equal, ignoring the totalizing hierarchal worldviews traditionally used to organize knowledge into a single comprehensive system. The innovation at prediction markets is not the mechanism but the decision to invert the relationship between money and information, subordinating the former to the pursuit of the latter. In other words, the ability to generate wisdom from these crowds depends on seeing wisdom as a bottom-up social product rather than as top-down content from authorities.

Of course, there are dangers on this path; many have already been identified. We rely on search engines to tell us what's important, even though bloggers are the Web's most prolific and timely linkers and have a disproportionate role in shaping search engine results. We resort to a free, all-volunteer online encyclopedia for quick research, even though anyone who actually knows a topic also knows that these articles just pass muster. We publish just about anything online because the near-zero cost has displaced the substantive question Why publish? with the rhetorical question Why not publish? We cut and paste our way through the Web's vast resources, as if everything were miscellaneous, even though we know that nuggets of information, taken out of their contexts, have lost most of their meaning and that our power browsing, a mile wide and an inch deep, is not at all the same as analysis and inference. Some even say we are losing our capacity for the concentrated attention that reading an actual book requires as well as our taste for the interior pleasures of self-reflection, contemplation and imagination. All these dangers are quite real.

Similarly, all knowledge always was and will be socially produced; that's not new. But we have entered an age in which tools are readily available that enable us to engineer that social production, and we certainly are figuring out how to process our thoughts with machines to yield relevant discoveries, reliable probabilities and perhaps other cognitive outputs in the future. Whether our engineering of collective intelligence is put to better uses that selecting CDs or predicting sales, time will tell. As long as the barriers are low, experimentation is likely to broaden. What's already certain is that, going forward, more of what each of us knows will be anchored directly and explicitly in what all of us know, presented with the authority of the crowd and a freshness date.

Notes

1 See Howard Rheingold, *The Virtual Community: Homesteading on the Electronic Frontier* (Reading: Addison-Wesley, 1993).

2 See Clay Skirky, *Here Comes Everybody: The Power of Organizing without Organizations* (New York: Penguin, 2008). Shirky rightly emphasizes that mobile devices that can transmit to and from the Web are central in enabling groups to coordinate and collaborate as well as share content.

3 Pierre Levy, *Collective Intelligence: Mankind's Emerging World in Cyberspace* (New York: Plenum, 1997).

4 Kevin Kelly, "Evidence of a SuperOrganism" The Technium, October 24, 2008, www.kk.org/thetechnium/archives/ 2008/10/ evidence_of_a_g.php, which reprises themes from his *Out of Control: The New Biology of Machines, Social Systems and the Economic World* (Reading: Addison-Wesley, 1994).

5 Tim O'Reilly, "What is Web 2.0?" O'Reilly, September 30, 2005, http://oreilly.com/web2/archive/what-is-web-20.html.

6 The topography of networks using one-way links and fixed nodes is explained in this book's introduction.

7 Some projects look like worksourcing but aren't. The University of Washington, for example, created an online game called *Fold It* in which players compete in folding proteins, but the goal is to gain insights into the human brain's abilities at pattern recognition and apply the insights to improving protein-generating software. In short, *Fold It* is research. Worksourcing must also be distinguished from distributed computing projects in which idle computers are accessed to process data. The best known is the search for extraterrestrial intelligence pursued by SETI@home, run by the University of California, Berkeley. Volunteers download the SETI@home software; when their computers are idle, the software automatically downloads a "work unit" of radio telescope data, performs a "signal analysis" and returns the analyzed findings. Over 5 million computer users in more than 200 countries have contributed over 19 billion hours of processing time. Such distributed computing projects harvest processing power; humans and human intelligence are not involved.

8 Cornelia Dean, "If You Have a Problem, Ask Everyone," *The New York Times,* (July 22, 2008, www.nytimes.com/2008/07/22/science/22inno.html.

9 Scott Page, *The Difference: How the Power of Diversity Creates Better Groups, Firms, Schools and Society* (Princeton: Princeton University Press, 2007).

10 The positive assessments of collaborative content creation derive in part from the contrast with traditional methods. See Yochai Benkler, *The Wealth of Networks: How Social Production Transforms Markets and Freedom* (New Haven: Yale University Press, 2007) for legal and economic perspectives. Charles Leadbeater, *We-Think: Mass Innovation, Not Mass Production: The Power of Mass Creativity* (London: Profile Books, 2008) offers an assessment from the bottom up.

11 Information filters such as spam blockers remove items flowing to the user; recommender systems add items flowing toward the user.

12 Cross-system collaborative filtering, where a user's filters from multiple recommender systems are combined, has been implemented but has not yet gained public acceptance.

13 Like all research based on expressed responses, those who contribute responses, either voluntarily or on request, are not necessarily representative of the larger population.

14 Robin Hanson, "The Informed Press Favored the Policy Analysis Market" (August 8, 2005), http://hanson.gmu.edu/PAMpress.pdf.

15 A brief expert summary of social network analysis is "Social Network Analysis: A Brief Introduction," www.orgnet.com/sna.html. John Seely Brown and Paul Duguid, *The Social Life of Information* (Cambridge, MA: Harvard Business School Publishing Corporation, 2000) and Marleen Huysman and Volker Wulf, *Social Capi-*

tal and Information Technology (Cambridge, MA: The MIT Press, 2004) are notable analyses. The intersection of prediction markets and social network analysis is explored by Bo Cowgill, Justin Wolfers, Eric Zitzewitz, "Using Prediction Markets to Track Information Flows: Evidence from Google," http://www.bocowgill.com/GooglePredictionMarketPaper.pdf.

16 Martin Spann and Bernd Skiera, "Internet-Based Virtual Stock Markets for Business Forecasting," *Management Science* 49 (October 2003), 1,310—1,226 offers a technical assessment of the accuracy of prediction markets in business contexts.

17 See Renee Dye, "The Promise of Prediction Markets," *McKinsey Quarterly*, no. 2 (2008) for Google's uses, Michael Totty, "How to Decide. Create a Market," *Wall Street Journal*, June 19, 2006 for applications at General Electric and Hewlett-Packard and Phred Dvorak, "Best Buy Taps Prediction Market," *Wall Street Journal*, September 16, 2008. The uses by the unnamed top-10 pharmaceutical company is based on an unpublished presentation.

18 Barnaby Feder, "To Learn What People Like, Trade 'Idea Stocks'," *The New York Times*, February 10, 2002. For a detailed description of MIT's Virtual Customer project and its aspiration to revolutionize product development, see "Virtual Consumer," MIT Sloan Management, http://mitsloan.mit.edu/vc/. On the traditional statistical procedures for this analytic task, see John Jullens and Gregor Harter, "Tracking the Elusive Consumer," *Strategy + Business Resilience Report*, November 11, 2008, www.strategy-business.com/media/file/resilience-11-11-08.pdf.

19 This binary outcome format has proven effective in generating predictions that closely approximate actual results and is the most widely used format. See David M. Pennock et al., "The Real Power of Artificial Markets," *Science*, February 2001, 987—988. It should also be noted that the settlement date can be implicit, such as "Candidate A will win the election."

20 Charles F. Manski, "Interpreting the Predictions of Prediction Markets," August 2005, www.aeaweb.org/annual_mtg_papers/2006/0106_1015_0703.pdf and Justin Wolfers and Eric Zitzewitz, "Interpreting Prediction Market Prices as Probabilities," January 8, 2007, http://bpp.wharton.upenn.edu/jwolfers/Papers/InterpretingPredictionMarketPrices.pdf provide mathematical assessments of using trading prices as a stand-in for probabilities.

21 Jennifer Watkins, "Prediction Markets as an Aggregation Mechanism for Collective Intelligence," (speech, 2007 UCLA Lake Arrowhead Human Complex Systems Conference, April 25–29, 2007) http://repositories.cdlib.org/hcs/WorkingPapers2/JHW2007 is a particularly clear exposition of these requirements. James Surowiecki, *The Wisdom of Crowds* (New York: Anchor, 2005) emphasizes how hard and rare it is to get everything right.

22 To be accurate, the commodity exchanges enable companies to hedge against price changes in raw materials as well as enable traders to speculate.

23 The use of money as an incentive is not, however, necessary for prediction markets to generate accurate results; see Emile Servan-Schreiber et al., "Prediction Markets: Does Money Matter," *Electronic Markets*_14 (September 2004).

CONCLUSION

> What is appearance for me now? Certainly not the
> opposite of some essence: what could I say about any
> essence except to name the attributes of its appearance?
> —Friedrich Nietzsche, *The Gay Science* (1882)

In 1993 the *New Yorker* magazine ran a cartoon by Peter
Steiner in which one dog, sitting in front of a home computer,
says to another dog sitting beside him, "On the Internet
nobody knows you're a dog." The caption alluded to the
chat rooms and electronic bulletin boards of the text-only
pre-Web Internet where users, logged on under their screen
names, discussed topics of all sorts. Among the obvious benefits, then and now, ordinary folks in socially stigmatized situations, such as living with diabetes or filing for bankruptcy,
can get or give something helpful without disclosing their
real world identities. Even more broadly, ordinary folks in
ordinary situations, such as shopping for a car or finding new
dinner recipes, can get what they want without dealing with
salespeople or being obliged to reciprocate.[1] On the downside, the use of screen names enables sexual predators, con
artists and other deceivers to pretend to be someone they
are not.

Internet users are largely lackadaisical about our online
anonymity. Losing it would be a disaster, but few pay it attention. Large majorities tell pollsters that they are "concerned"
or "very concerned" about privacy online. In actuality, however, vast numbers of us give up our birthdays, zip codes and
other personally identifying data to any Web site that asks in
exchange for ringtones, screen savers, horoscopes and other
trinkets. Similarly, very few use the privacy-protecting tools
that have long been available. Leaking out personal data
has become just a routine feature of the contemporary consumer condition.

We have a greater stake in anonymity's opposite, authentication. Verifying one's identity is essential to every electronic transaction, offline and online, and the recent spread of terrorist attacks has made it essential to our physical safety as well. The obvious downside of authentication systems is identity theft. The increasing importance of verifiable identities may help in perceiving the emergence of our silicon simulacra, but they are very different. Authentication verifies us. Our simulations make us knowable; they turn us out in public to others, albeit inside machines.

I am a number!

Authentication dates back to the 1920s. It was one dimension of the in-house credit systems that department stores offered their good customers. Some people at the time were nervous about the gathering of personal information for these services, but convenience won out. Authentication became ubiquitous in the 1970s as plastic credit cards replaced cash in everyday purchases. We still don't know the details. We just know that every swipe sends the card number somewhere where it gets processed and then sent back, either approved or denied.[2] Similarly, when we register at Web sites, we know, sort of, that the valid e-mail address we provide is an individual identifier and that the password we provide verifies it. We resonate to the defiant protest, "I am not a number" as a cultural critique, but we accept that the great circuits know us as numbers, two numbers in particular.

The first is one's Social Security number or its equivalent, like the number of one's passport, military service ID or state-issued driver's license. Because these numbers are unique and assigned to individuals, they can verify that a person is who she claims to be and can function as keys to open and access accounts and dossiers. The other is one's credit score. Compiled by three consumer credit reporting agencies—Equifax, Experian and Transunion, this number is a rating; it compares each of us to others and on that basis grants access to other resources, usually more or less credit. Not long ago, a person's credit score was inaccessible. Today, consumers have a legal right to their credit reports for free at least once a year and can challenge and correct the information they contain. For a fee, consumers can also subscribe to services that will monitor and report on a daily, weekly or monthly basis which third parties are requesting one's credit score; one can even place certain access controls on such requests, including an outright freeze.

As authentication regimes grew prevalent, so did identity theft. We tolerate this downside but shouldn't. This crime *du jour* is not an inescapable consequence; rather, it reflects how informational rewards and risks are defined. The problem that gives rise to identity theft is the separation of rewards and risks: businesses get the rewards while consumers bear the risks.

Legally, no individual can be a victim of identity theft. Theft applies to property, and under U.S. law the individual has no property interest in her data. The companies that compile the data into databases have the property interest. In the landmark legal case, American Express was exonerated for selling its cardmembers' names to merchants because, the court argued, "an individual name has value only when associated with the defendant's lists." That is, by compiling and categorizing our personal information, the data aggregator creates the value that constitutes the property interest.

But the owners of this property have few incentives to protect it Although most states require companies to report data breaches and threaten to impose fines on those who don't, there are many holes. Some states require only businesses in certain industries to report while still other states require it only if the business suspects the stolen data will be used to commit fraud. What's more, even when fines are levied for failure to report a breach, they're small, much less than what it would cost to research and report a breach. So, many data thefts go unreported; it's cheaper to just pay the fine. In short, the downsides for property owners are minor if their property is stolen.

In contrast, the consumer becomes a victim when someone uses the stolen data to impersonate the consumer. That crime is not theft but fraud, and the harm is relatively major, usually charges against one's credit cards or, worse, entirely new credit card accounts and bank loans opened in one's name. In addition, significant time is required to repair the informational damage, that is, to correct one's records at banks, retailers, credit rating agencies and police departments. What's more, seeking compensation from the company whose security was breached is not viable because connecting the fraud back to the theft is difficult, usually impossible.

This disconnect—businesses get the rewards while consumers get the risks—encourages both theft from the former and fraud against the latter. Rather than address the cause, we're letting the marketplace address the effects by asking prospective victims to pay in advance for protection. Quite concretely, consumer services for identity protection and credit monitoring are flourishing businesses.

While Americans have long been comfortable in being individually verified as consumers, the terrorist attacks of September 11, 2001 have made authentication necessary for us as citizens as well. The age of terror has made anonymity problematic and intensified a classic dilemma: government surveillance to ensure our collective security encroaches upon individual privacy. Immediately after 9/11, for example, the Defense Department wanted to datamine all the transaction records of everyone in the country, looking for tell-tale patterns of terrorist plotting, while the U.S. Attorney General wanted to allow the FBI not only to conduct surveillance outside specific investigations but also to compile dossiers about individuals who participate in public assemblies and who visit certain Web sites.

The government's track record isn't good here. Back in the 1950s, '60s and into the '70s, the FBI used its surveillance capabilities to undermine legitimate political activity, including both the civil rights and anti-war movements. But no government's track record was or ever will be good here. The peril is inherent and the Founding Fathers knew it. From the grievances listed in the Declaration of Independence to the checks and balances built into the Constitution to the individual freedoms secured by the Bill of Rights, all our charter documents focus on protecting us against the ever-present temptation of governments to encroach upon the rights of those they are supposed to protect.

Whenever the watchdogs bark, we should listen, but our need for increased security must also be addressed. Defending individual privacy against government surveillance is necessary; it keeps the tension healthy, but it does not solve the dilemma. Nor is the solution to demand anonymity in public life. Freedom means little if its exercise requires anonymity. Rather, we have freedoms of speech and assembly to the extent that we can stand up and be counted without fear of sanctions.

Not the right to privacy but the duty of publicity applies here. The American jurist Louis Brandeis coined both phrases. The latter means that people have a right to know who is addressing them and that speakers have a duty to be accountable. The sunlight of others' approbation exercises a disciplining pressure. Anonymity removes it. As many know from online discussion forums, anonymity facilitates all sorts of disruptive and destructive behaviors. From our experience of computer systems generally, many also know the opposite, presenting a valid ID grants access to whatever resources one is entitled. "Enrollment enables entitlement" is a well-known motto in computer security circles. In the wake of 9/11, we've all grown accustomed not only to more surveillance but also to presenting some form of official identification whenever we try to cross some threshold, online and offline, and gain access to whatever's on the other side. In balancing safety and privacy, our willingness to be individually authenticated is emerging as the way forward.

The rise of identity theft and our response to terrorism have made us aware that each of us has identities that machines can read. These identifiers make us safer by authenticating us; at the same time they render us vulnerable to impersonation and fraud. Identity is not individuality, however, and authenticating the one does not disclose the other. Under authentication regimes, we remain private individuals. Our silicon simulacra, the data profile and the cyberpersona, are different. They make us visible and knowable as individuals to others.

The New Publicity

In general, Americans don't go in much for public life. We don't have the pub cultures of northern Europe or the sidewalk social life of cafes and bistros common in the olive zone. As for our home-grown civic associations, fraternal orders, business clubs, ladies' auxiliaries and other formally organized groups, they've long since faded away. Americans may have once been a nation of joiners, but today we bowl alone. Indeed, it is a common complaint that Americans lead largely privatized lives.

Both the datascape and cyberspace, however, want us knowable. Although the former relies largely on surveillance while the latter promotes self-disclosure, the end result is the same. Both subvert the essence of the Romantic self—mysterious, quixotic and out of reach—and replace it with a self that is knowable, present in the here and now and open to entrance by others.

In the datascape such visibility enables those with power—governments, businesses and employers—to make ever-more precise decisions that benefit themselves rather than citizens, consumers and employees. Cyberspace is similar. Every Web 2.0 application invites each of us to make our activities, interests, tastes, preferences, expertise and predictions available and knowable to others, including marketers who buy our eyeballs and foot the bill for these free applications.

But the ways in which we become knowable inside each machine differ and not in the ways many would expect.

Contrary to the concerns of privacy champions, the datascape does not threaten individuals. Individuals with our qualities and possibilities don't even get into databases; we're left outside. Only machine-readable attributes make their way in, and, once inside, they just sit idle as raw material until someone queries the database. Only then is the raw material processed. Those real-life people whose attributes conform to the query become the hypothetical persons of the data profile. This is a probabilistic informational entity: a set of persons who are statistically predicted to be more likely than others to conform to some specific end state desired by some marketer, bureaucrat or other planner. On that basis, it provides the scientific (read: objective and impartial) rationale for those decision makers to treat some of us differently than others. To be sure, statistical differentiation for commercial discrimination affects us individuals. Some of us get treated better than others, but that happens to us as members of groups. Individuals are not at risk. Rather, the direct impacts of this decision-making regime are largely social. Three are especially problematic.

First and foremost, while using data to understand and govern human affairs accomplishes a world of good, it does not capture our qualities or our possibilities. The omission has two consequences. Ersatz versions of us go into databases, and the ersatz answers about us that come out are the basis for marketers, bureaucrats and other planners to make decisions about nearly every inch of the built environment in which we live. The built environment produced by their decisions fits the data well enough but doesn't quite fit the humans from whom the data was abstracted. The second consequence of this omission is worse. The more data is used to apprehend and administer human affairs, the more it tends to push into the shadows other traditions that do address our qualities and possibilities. This surreptitious coercion into cultural amnesia could be characterized as ideological because the hallmark of any ideology is to prescind alternative ways of apprehending the world. Ideological or not, this systematic forgetting disadvantages us in trying to make sense or meaning of our lives.

The second social problem derives from the one overarching purpose of all data-based decision making, to create and measure difference. Differences are not natural. Specific decision makers hypothesize specific differences for their specific purposes; they then create variables that ostensibly express those differences, collect observations and analyze the results. Whatever we have in common is of no use to them because it cannot support a decision to allocate resources here *rather than* there. So they never look for what we share or may want to share. Only difference is hypothesized, only difference comes out and only difference is made real via the data-based decisions about the built environment. Whatever the specific differences hypothesized in any particular instance and whatever one thinks of those differences, a society centered on the cultivation of difference is going to have a hard time figuring out how to move forward together, at home or abroad.

The third socially problematic aspect is the rarely discussed vision of the larger society within which difference is framed. That vision sees society as a socioeconomic stratification system in which the established hierarchy of power and interests are givens. Although this framework suits the purposes of those who own, operate and utilize the apparatus, it's only one way of seeing our society. Moreover, it omits several socioeconomic changes of historical magnitude that actually challenge us today and, like all feedback systems, is self-reinforcing and self-perpetuating. In short, the framework locks us into the past and tends to preempt different visions of the social fabric.

All three consequences—the cultural amnesia, the cultivation of difference and the outdated vision of the hierarchal whole—are social in their substance. They set up the world in which we live, and their impacts register in the built environment. Data profiles are the imagined persons for whom the built environment is built. They flourish in the datascape. Indeed, each of us is transformed into profiles thousands of times every day. But they're informational entities, not individuals.

In contrast, our cyberpersonas make us public as highly articulated individuals and do so not through surveillance but through our voluntary self-disclosure. Unlike our passive contributions to the data profile, mostly the electronic traces of our shopping and buying, we actively create our cyberpersonas through the content we publish and through the connections we make with others. The content we publish is our online presence. What others think of our content's quality, expressed by their links and clicks to that content, is our online reputation. Presence and reputation make us visible and knowable as individuals.

This persona-generating self-disclosure has three substantial benefits for the user. Self-expression is one. Anyone can now easily and inexpensively publish content they create, including content whose narrow appeal would not meet marketplace requirements. (Many use the opportunity for personal updates, gossip and sociable chatter, but some, a large number in absolute terms, publish pro bono technical treatises, thoughtful commentaries and other meaningful content on substantive topics.) The second benefit is the change in the relationship of reader and author. Our cyberpersonas are in part co-created with others in the give and take of online conversations. In this process, readers are also authors and vice versa. Third, users can ignore official worldviews. By inserting links of their own choosing and applying tags of their own devising, they can organize and present content, user-generated and otherwise, according to their own worldviews. Our persona-generating activity makes use of all three.

Much of this activity focuses on our lives as consumers. This is explicit by definition in the user-managed interfaces for the "virtual consumer" and at the product review sites,

but it's pervasive across the Web 2.0 terrain. Our social network profiles, personal blog posts and a large portion of the
images we upload to file-hosting sites are filled with our tastes
in music, books and movies, with details of our hobbies and
vacations, with snapshots of the concerts and sports events
we go to, with links to the bars and restaurants we like, and so
on. So, too, among the collective intelligence applications,
most rating, ranking and recommendation systems are designed to filter the vast inventories of cultural commodities
available for our consumption.

This emphasis is predictable and unobjectionable. Everyone's everyday life involves a good deal of shopping and
buying, and each of us finds some self-expression in what
we buy and how we consume what we buy. What's remark-
able about the cyberpersona is its highly individuated content, and all the services and applications through which we
generate that persona are designed to facilitate it. The virtual consumer interfaces assume we are not merely willing
but eager to make our particular wants and needs known
to the marketplace. In the Web 2.0 terrain, the social network sites build in functionalities that enable us to share our
friends, tastes, interests and activities. Blogs enable us to
share our thoughts; the software envisions a personal journal, a window onto the mind of the blogger that's open to
others. The images we post to file-hosting sites are literally
our views of the world, just as the tags we use at bookmarking sites express our particular worldviews. The collective intelligence applications do not by definition result
in self-disclosure, but even their outputs require that we
reveal our preferences and predictions to their processing
machinery.

Our self-disclosure via these applications—biographical
information on our schooling, careers and family lives, updates on our hobbies, indicators of our tastes, preferences
and loyalties, snapshots of the public and private events we
attend, the topics that interest us and our opinions about
them—makes privacy defenders cringe. Their paradigm

assumes we want to withhold ourselves from view. Cyberpersona assumes that we want to advance ourselves into view and do so in the highly articulated form of this and no other individual.

So far, users have asserted only two claims to their online representations. One, we want to control its publicity, that is, which portions of our self-presentation are shared with whom and under what circumstances. Two, we want to take both our content and our connections with us wherever we go on the Web. User claims to the publicity and portability of our cyberpersonas are likely just the beginning. As more of our everyday lives occurs or is replicated online, our presence and reputation online will likely evince additional dimensions and dynamics, the control of which will be in the user's interest.

Whatever dimensions and dynamics emerge, advancing any claim as a matter of "right" is always a complicated effort. It may be more effective to advance claims to our cyberpersonas as "wants" that the marketplace can fill. This could work. The Web is still a fluid medium, very much a work in progress, and Web developers have proven adept at putting users in the driver's seat and letting user behavior guide product evolution. Just as important, many more users will be confronting these matters head-on. As more of our everyday lives occurs or is replicated online, our presence and reputation will grow without our active oversight or cultivation. However, to the extent that a coherent and compelling cyberpersona becomes an increasingly important social asset and an increasingly widespread social expectation, each of us will have to take up with self-conscious purpose the tasks of building, managing and making good use of our online presence and reputation. In other words, whether we advance our claims to our cyberpersonas as rights or as wants, they will likely become responsibilities for most of us. There's only one catch: as a hybrid entity the cyberpersona like the data profile has features with which we are unfamiliar.

Post-Human Entities

Although data profile and cyber-persona make us public in different ways, both are hybrid entities. They are part human. Carbon-based individuals provide the raw material in continuous flows for both. As we change, our simulations change in tandem. They are part machine. The machine determines what we can put into it and how whatever we put in is then served up to others.

The datascape is a mathematical world, and the profile is made of data, comparable and combinable values on common attributes that are processed into probabilities. Cyberspace is a network world, and the persona is made of connections, the links and clicks that we make to others and they make to us. Probability and pattern are the forms in which human raw material appears inside these two machines. Both have features that don't seem to fit the humans from whom they are derived. While the individuated being that each of us experiences is a continuous, whole and bounded entity, our simulacra are contingent, relative and open to others. Indeed, our machine appearances are hard to pin down.

Individuals persist from one moment to the next; that continuousness is our internal subjectivity and our external biography. In contrast, profile and persona do not even exist until they're called up. In the datascape, our attributes sit idle until someone queries the database. In cyberspace, content by or about us sits idle on a server until someone links or clicks to it. To be sure, their life spans differ. The profile is ephemeral; thousands are churned out and thrown away daily. The persona is forever; one's online fragments, wherever they appear, never disappear. Neither profile nor persona can conjure up themselves, however. Someone else must call them up.

Both simulations are always partial, because in every instance they are called up relative to the observer. In the datascape, the query determines the profile. The mind's eye of the beholder envisions a desired end state. The machinery then sorts through our attributes, and its mathematics call up into the profile only those attributes that contribute in a statistically significant way to the end state envisioned by the query. Thus, every profile portrays us as an object of desire defined by the eye of the beholder. Similarly, cyberpersona is partial because relative but in a network way. Each of us has digital fragments by or about us in various locations across the Web, but the Web is not a lattice of evenly spaced nodes. It's an irregular mesh of knotted and clustered connections, created by the preferential attachments of its users. Which of anyone's fragments become visible to whom depends on the observer's location in the network and the links he encounters and can traverse from that location. Unless the user claims and gathers all his fragments in one spot, our cyberpersonas are not visible in toto. They too are always partial because always relative to the location of the beholder on the network.

Finally, both simulations are open to others. The ability to combine and divide data enables decision makers to expand and narrow the scope of human affairs about which they assert knowledge. In the datascape, they continually reconfigure us with varying others to optimize our utility to their desired end states. The data profile has boundaries, but they are always provisional. Cyberpersona is open in its way; it depends on the "other." The virtual consumer requires the online merchant; they co-create. The social network profile requires friends for its existence; in fact, the activities of those friends provide most of the content of the profile owner's page. So, too, bloggers are visible only to readers; indeed, blogging becomes dynamic only when readers comment, turning posts into conversations. Similarly, whatever collective intelligence is created by those applications that enable us to think together is by definition co-created by their users.

Contingent, relative and open to others, our simulacra seem different from the continuous, whole and bounded individual from whom they are derived. Among the many

ways one could characterize this divergence, three contemporary perspectives are useful to spell out: the post-modern,
the post-humanist and the post-human. They take different
paths to the same place.

The post-modern view dismisses the continuous, whole
and bounded self as a modernist fiction. The internal world
each of us knows subjectively has always been a social construct, created from within language and our situations. In
this view the hero of modernism including the individuated
"in here" has always been contingent, relative and open.

The post-humanist view also sees this autonomous being as a modernist fiction with strengths and weaknesses, cultural and scientific, all of which we can now move beyond.
Instead, we should understand the self as including and even
give preeminence to our permanently partial identities, the
contradictory standpoints from which they appear and the
continuous co-authoring of them through interacting with
others. These attributes of the more broadly conceived post-
humanist self are similar to those proposed for the more
narrowly conceived post-human entity with one obvious difference: the post-human view doesn't bother with the hero
of modernism.

From a cybernetic perspective, the post-human is an informational entity, continually nourished by the carbon-based
world but disembodied and shaped for silicon-based worlds.
Transposing human affairs into data is how we are disembodied and move from carbon into silicon. The resulting
entity inside the machine lacks the boundaries, coherence
and destiny of singular individuals. Instead, it is composed
of heterogeneous components that are subject to continuous
construction and reconstruction and that manifest different
identities under different perspectives.

This cybernetic concept captures at a high level the contexts in which the simulations discussed here arose, the features they have in common and our relationship to them.
They are not our descendants, successors or representatives;
rather, they are simulations of us, nourished by our lives but

shaped and served up to others by the machines in which they appear. For all the undeniable benefits that data profiles and cyberpersonas deliver, these simulations are human-machine hybrids and as novel entities merit our wary attention. As Norbert Weiner, the founder of cybernetics explained at its outset, "What is used as an element in a machine is in fact an element in a machine." That's both an observation and a caution.

Notes

1 On the benefit of avoiding obligations, see Thomas Erickson, "The World Wide Web as Social Hypertext" at http://www.pliant. org/personal/Tom_Erickson/SocialHpertext.html. Anonymity also removes the "shadow of the future" from our interactions with others. This concept refers to the following behavior-governing expectation: I act toward you today in the expectation that you will act toward me likewise tomorrow

2 Joe Arena, "Framing an Ideology of Information: Retail Credit and the Mass Media, 1910-1930," *Media, Culture and Society* vol. 18 (1996), pp. 423-445 explains retail credit extracted the individual's trustworthiness from local social networks and quantified into a number, making it portable and comparable.

APPENDIX I

DATA PROFILES: SUPPRESSION LISTS

No one can escape the datascape. The government wants each of us tagged at birth with a Social Security number, and it captures additional data when we get a driver's license, register to vote, buy or sell property, get married or divorced, have a baby, file for unemployment insurance, pay taxes, appear in court or in any other way get involved with any government bureaucracy. As for the marketplace, unless you pay in cash, every swipe of a plastic card leaves a trace; so do catalog purchases, telephone orders, Web site transactions, warranty cards, mail-in rebates, sweepstakes entries et al., and marketers want all of it.

To be fair, consumers do get some direct benefits in the "primary information market," that is, from the companies that consumers deal with directly, usually retailers and service companies. The average U.S. household, for example, saves about $200 a year from using a supermarket's frequent-shopper program. Airline frequent flyer and hotel frequent guest points, when redeemed, yield discounts ranging from 1 percent to 5 percent of the prices paid by non-members.[1] It's meager but still it's coin.

These companies also sell portions of their customers' information into the "secondary information market" where it is combined with other consumer data sets and then sold to other companies with which the consumer has not dealt directly and for purposes unknown to the consumer. The only direct benefit here is the greater relevance of the commercial messages that consumers receive from strangers.

To get out of the secondary information market, one must actively opt out of it, and to do so comprehensively requires that one de-list one's name in several ways. First, the industry's trade group, the Direct Marketing Association, offers consumers just such "suppression" services. It's not illogical. Opting-out contributes to what the business calls data hygiene. By deleting names of those who have no interest in receiving their solicitations, direct marketers get cleaner lists and better returns on their mailing costs. Consumers get less junk in their mailboxes while reducing their traces in the datascape.

To be thorough, consumers can also remove their names from the lists offered for sale by the four major list brokers, but each must be contacted directly.

Getting off the lists for pre-approved or pre-screened offers of credit cards and insurance policies is a special case. Under the Fair Credit Reporting Act (FCRA), only four companies—Equifax, Experian, TransUnion and Innovis—are permitted to include a consumer's name on lists used by lenders or insurers to make these unsolicited firm offers. FCRA requires that consumers be able to opt out from these lists, and the four companies maintain a common suppression-list service that prevents all of them from providing credit file information for such offers.

The credit card companies also sell their cardholders' names into the secondary information market, and cardholders can get off those lists as well. American Express is a standalone operation, and its customer service department will remove a member's name upon request from its in-house lists, outside company lists or both. For Visa and MasterCard, the cardholder has to contact the bank, credit union or other financial institution that issued the card and ask it not to sell, trade or lend one's name and address to any organization for its mailing lists.

Warranty cards are a primary fuel of the list business. They are not, however, required for a product to be covered by a warranty, and the only benefit to consumers is finding out about product recalls. To get these notices, the warranty card need only include the purchaser's name and address and the product's serial number. All the other information is used by the manufacturer for additional marketing purposes or sold in the secondary information market to other companies; it need not be included.

The online world poses different challenges. Here, consumers need to protect their computers from identity thieves, and we're not doing a very good job of it. We underestimate the extent to which our computers are infected by viruses and spyware, and too few of us install the firewalls, filters and other applications than can help protect our hardware from such invasions. Clearly, each of us needs to do a better job at securing our nodes on the network.

Once out in cyberspace, the safest practice is not to do anything. Don't download any freebies, don't install any applications on your toolbar, don't subscribe to any newsletters and so on. There is no free lunch. To get something requires giving something, usually data. Sometimes the request is explicit, such as filling out a registration page on a Web site; sometimes it's tacit, such as giving permission to have a cookie installed on one's browser, a small string of computer code that enables Web sites to recognize that browser each time it visits. Consumers can opt out of having their cookie data shared among online advertisers, courtesy of the Network Advertising Initiative, and can even surf the Web anonymously, but leaving fewer traces diminishes some of the Web's chief benefits.

We want Amazon to know, analyze and share what items we buy because we benefit when Amazon tells us that others who bought this item also bought these other items. Google uses the search terms and click-through histories of its users to deliver more relevant search results. We want our playlists on Rhapsody and Last.fm open for browsing and crunching because only by contributing our taste preferences do we train our own filters and get recommendations for similar musical artists. Users can opt out and withhold their data, but the Web would become less useful for them and the rest of us.

The general rules for the online and offline worlds, then, are opposite: Online, don't opt out of anything you don't have to. Offline, unless there's a direct and worthwhile benefit, opt out of everything you can. The following page provides contact information for the services that will suppress one's name and address from the lists used in offline mailings.

Notes

1 "Selling Your Personal Data: Interview with John Deighton," CNET News.com, September 1, 2003, http://news.cnet.com/2030-1069_3-5068504.html is the source for these estimated savings.

SUPPRESSION LIST SERVICES

Mail

General
Direct Marketing Association
www.dmachoice.org

Mailing Lists
Database America
Compilation Department
470 Chestnut Ridge Road
Woodcliff, NJ 07677

Dun & Bradstreet
Customer Service
899 Eaton Avenue
Bethlehem, PA 18025

Metromail Corporation
List Maintenance
901 West Bond
Lincoln, NE 68521

R.L. Polk
Name Deletion File
26955 Northwestern Hwy.
Southfield, MI 48034

Marketing Lists
Credit card/insurance offers
www.optoutprescreen.com

Catalog/magazine subscribers
Epsilon: abacusoptout@epsilon.com

Samples, coupons and flyers
Experian: 402-458-5247

Marketing, fundraising and surveys
Acxiom: optoutUS@acxiom.com

Varied
Equifax: 888-567-8688

E-mail
Direct Marketing Association
www.dmachoice.org

Cookie Sharing
Network Advertising Initiative
www.networkadvertising.org

APPENDIX II

CYBERPERSONA: MY URL

Registering at a Web site improves the user's experience on subsequent visits in two ways. The site recognizes the user and adjusts its content accordingly and, if it's an e-commerce site, the user doesn't have to fill out again her billing, shipping and contact information. At the same time two problems result. Most of us have registered at many sites, and one problem is remembering all our passwords. That's why every log-on page includes a "Forget Password?" link and why many use the same password to register everywhere. The other is keeping track of what subsets of our personal data we gave to the different Web sites at which we registered. The more we do online, the more complex this becomes.

The emerging technology that solves both is a distributed, or user-managed, identity. The most popular application currently is single sign-on. It provides the user with one logon that unlocks access to all the sites at which the user has registered and can automate registration at additional sites. Among these single sign on solutions, OpenID, a free and open-source application for distributed authentication, has gained traction. As of December 2009, more than 1 billion OpenIDs have been issued and more than 9 million sites support it.[1] Although most major sites, such as AOL, Google, Microsoft, MySpace and Yahoo, enable their visitors to sign up for OpenID, their sign-up pages are hard to find. The simpler path is to visit any of the specialized providers such as ClaimID, myOpenID, myID.net and VeriSign's Personal Identity Provider.

The one requirement for single sign-on is that each user have his own URL, the address of a Web page or blog that belongs to the user. The site or blog need not contain a single word. The URL just has to be owned by the user, so it can be used to authenticate the user as this and no other user. It can perform this authentication function because acquiring a URL from any of the Internet's domain-name registrars requires providing a valid real world mailing and billing address.   (In contrast, the valid e-mail address used to register at Web sites is easily faked and, so, cannot authenticate.) With a user-owned URL as the online authenticator of the user's offline identity, users can register at the people search engines and presence aggregators and start claiming the online content that's by or about the user.

Although the people search engines will spider the Web for mentions of one's name, a comprehensive search requires several narrower services as well. Backtype, Samepoint and Socialmention round up references from social network sites, blogs, wikis and social bookmarking sites. Technorati and Blogsearch specialize in scouring the blogosphere. Entering one's name in Google News returns any mentions in news articles and press releases. Finally, Bigboards and Google Groups will search the discussion forums. Once all mentions are gathered up, they can be compiled into one or more coherent self-presentations and shared selectively via the people engines. But to exist on the Web, the first step for the individual, and anything else, for that matter, is to get a URL of one's own.

Notes

1 Brian Kissel, "OpenID 2009 Year in Review" December 16, 2009, http://openid.net/2009/12/16/openid-2009-year-in-review/.

BIBLIOGRAPHY

Armano, David. "Friendship Isn't Dead: The Strengthening of Loose Ties." Logic + Emotion (March 19, 2009): http://darmano.typepad.com/logic_emotion/2009/03/friendship-isnt-dead-the-strengthening-of-loose-ties.html.

Barabási, Albert-László. *Linked: The New Science of Networks.* Cambridge, MA: Perseus Publishing, 2002.

Bate, Walter Jackson. *From Classic to Romantic: Premises of Taste in Eighteenth Century England.* New York: Harper & Row, 1961.

Bell, Daniel. *The Coming of Post-Industrial Society: A Venture in Social Forecasting.* New York: Harper Colophon, 1973.

———. "The Social Framework of the Information Society." In *The Computer Age: A Twenty-Year View,* edited by Michael I. Dertouzos and Joel Moses. Cambridge, MA: MIT Press, 1979.

Beniger, James. *The Control Revolution: Technological and Economic Origins of the Information Society.* Cambridge, MA: Harvard University Press, 1986.

Benkler, Yochai. *The Wealth of Networks: How Social Production Transforms Markets and Freedom.* New Haven: Yale University Press, 2007.

Berlin, Isaiah. *Vico & Herder: Two Studies in the History of Ideas.* New York: Vintage, 1977.

Bloch, Ernst. "Man (sic) as Possibility." *Cross Currents* vol. 18 (1968): 273–283.

Blood, Rebecca. *The Weblog Handbook: Practical Advice on Creating and Maintaining Your Blog.* Cambridge, MA: Perseus, 2002.

Boorstin, Daniel J. *The Image: A Guide to Pseudo-Events in America.* New York: Harper & Row, 1961.

Bowker, Geoffrey C. and Susan Leigh Starr. *Sorting Things Out: Classification and Its Consequences.* Cambridge, MA: The MIT Press, 1999.

Bowra, C. M. *The Romantic Imagination*. Oxford: Oxford University Press, 1969.

boyd, danah m. "Controlling Your Public Appearance." Apophenia (September 7, 2007): www.zephoria.org/thoughts/archives/2007/09/07.

——— and Nicole B. Ellison. "Social Network Sites: Definition, History and Scholarship." *Journal of Computer-Mediated Communication 13*(1) (2007): article 11, http://jcmc.indiana.edu/vol13/issue1/boyd.ellison.html.

Buchanan, Margo-Oliver and David Redmore. "Trust-Based Customer Information Management (CIM) in the Network Economy: A Strategic Approach" (2002). IMP Group. www.impgroup.org/paper_view.php?viewPaper=497.

Burnett, Ron. *How Images Think* Cambridge, MA: The MIT Press, 2004.

Cameron, Kim, "Introduction to the Laws of Identity". IdentityBlog (January 8, 2006): www.identityblog.com/?p=354.

Campbell, Colin. *The Romantic Ethic and the Spirit of Modern Consumerism*. Cambridge, MA: Blackwell, 1987.

Cohen, Patricia Cline. *A Calculating People: The Spread of Numeracy in Early America*. New York: Routledge, 1999.

Cohen-Cole, Ethan. "Credit Card Redlining." Working Paper No. QAU08-1, Federal Reserve Bank of Boston, February 26, 2008.

Cook, Scott. "The Contribution Revolution: Letting Volunteers Build Your Business." *Harvard Business Review* October 2008.

Corcoran, Sean. "Add Sponsored Conversations to Your Toolbox: Why You Should Pay Bloggers to Talk about Your Brand." *Forrester Research* March 2, 2009.

Cummins, Walter. "Love and Liqueur: Modernism and Postmodernism in Advertising and Fiction." In *Advertising and Culture: Theoretical Perspectives* edited by Mary Cross. Westport, CT: Praeger, 1996.

Curtis, Terry. "The Information Society: A Computer-Generated Caste System." In *The Political Economy of Information* edited by Vincent Mosco and Janet Wasko. Madison, WI: University of Wisconsin Press, 1988.

Dean, Cornelia. "If You Have a Problem, Ask Everyone." *The New York Times.* July 22, 2008.

Deighton, John, "Marketing Solutions to Privacy Problems." HBS Working Paper abstract. www.hbs.edu/research/facpubs/workingpapers/abstracts/0203/03-024.html.

———, "Selling Your Personal Data: Interview with John Deighton." CNET News.com September 1, 2003: http://news.cnet.com/2030-1069_3-5068504.html.

De Rosnay, Joel. *The Symbiotic Man: A New Understanding of the Organization of Life and a Vision of the Future.* New York: McGraw-Hill, 2000.

Dooley, Roger. "Anonymous Reviews Headed for Extinction." Marketing Strategy and Innovation (December 6, 2008): www.futurelab.net/blogs/marketing-strategy-innovation/2008/12/anonymous_reviews_headed_for_e.html.

Drucker, Peter F. *Post-Capitalist Society.* New York: HarperCollins, 1993.

Duncan, Otis Dudley. *Notes on Social Measurement: Historical & Critical.* New York: Russell Sage Foundation, 1984.

Esslin, Martin. "Aristotle and the Advertisers: The Television Commercial Considered as a Form of Drama." In *Television: The Critical View* edited by Horace Newcomb. New York: Oxford University Press, 1987.

Featherstone, Mike. *Consumer Culture and Postmodernism.* London: Sage Publications, 1991.

———. "Lifestyle and Consumer Culture." *Theory, Culture and Society* vol. 4 (1987): 55–70.

Feder, Barnaby. "To Learn What People Like, Trade 'Idea Stocks.'" *The New York Times,* February 10, 2002.

Frank, Tom. *The Conquest of Cool: Business Culture, Counterculture and the Rise of Hip Consumerism.* Chicago: University of Chicago Press, 1997.

Galloway, Alexander R. *Protocol: How Control Exists After Decentralization.* Cambridge, MA: The MIT Press, 2004.

Gandy, Oscar H. "It's discrimination, stupid!" In *Resisting the Virtual Life: The Culture and Politics of Information* edited by J. Brook and I. Boal. San Francisco: City Lights Books, 1995.

———. "The Political Economy of Communications Competence." In *The Political Economy of Information* edited by Vincent Mosco and Janet Wasko. Madison, WI: University of Wisconsin Press, 1988.

Gauzente, Claire and Ashok Rachhod. "Ethical Marketing for Competitive Advantage on the Internet." *Academy of Marketing Science Review* vol. 2001, no. 10 2001.

Gelernter, David. *Mirror Worlds or the Day Software Puts the Universe in a Shoebox...How It Will Happen and What It Will Mean.* New York: Oxford University Press, 1991.

Gergen, Kenneth. *The Saturated Self: Dilemmas of Identity in Contemporary Life.* New York: Basic Books, 1991.

Gigerenzer, Gard et al. *The Empire of Chance: How Probability Changed Science and Everyday Life.* Cambridge, U.K.: Cambridge University Press, 1989.

Goody, Jack. *The Domestication of the Savage Mind.* London: Cambridge University Press, 1978.

Goss, John. "Marketing the New Marketing: The Strategic Discourse of Geodemographic Information Systems." In *Ground Truth: The Social Implications of Geographic Information Systems* edited by John Pickles. New York: Guilford Press, 1995.

Gouldner, Alvin W. *The Dialectic of Ideology and Technology: The Origins, Grammar and Future of Ideology.* New York: Oxford University Press, 1982.

Graham, Stephen. "Spaces of Surveillent-Simulation: New Technologies, Digital Representations and Material Geographies." *Environment and Planning: Society and Space* vol. 16 (1998): 483–504.

Hacking, Ian. *The Emergence of Probability: A Philosophical Study of Early Ideas about Probability, Induction and Statistical In-*

ference. Cambridge, U.K.: Cambridge University Press, 1975.

———. *The Taming of Chance.* New York: Cambridge University Press, 1990.

———. "Making People Up." In *Reconstructing Individualism: Autonomy, Individuality and the Self in Western Thought edited by* Thomas C. Heller et al. Stanford: Stanford University Press, 1986.

Hancock, Denis, "Crowdsourcing: Business Model Failure vs. Management Mistakes." Wikinomics (September 11, 2008): www.wikinomics.com/blog/index.php/2008/09/11/crowdsourcing-business-model-failure-vs-management-mistake/.

Hane, Paula J. "People Search Tools Populate the Web." *Information Today,* September 1, 2007, http://newsbreaks.infotoday.com/nbReader.asp?ArticleId=37403.

Hanson, Robin. "The Informed Press Favored the Policy Analysis Market" (August 8, 2005): http://hanson.gmu.edu/PAMpress.pdf.

Harraway, Donna. *Simians, Cyborgs, Women: The Reinvention of Nature.* New York: Routledge, 1991.

Harris, Will. "Why Web 2.0 will end your privacy." *Bit-techNet* (June 3, 2006): www.bit-tech.net/columns/2006/06/03/Web_2_privacy/1#top.

Harvey, David. *The Condition of Post-Modernity: An Enquiry into the Origins of Cultural Change.* Oxford, U.K.: Blackwell Publishing Ltd., 1990.

Hayles, N. Katherine. *How We Became Post-Human: Virtual Bodies in Cybernetics, Literature and Informatics.* Chicago: The University of Chicago Press, 1999.

Heidegger, Martin. *Basic Writings* edited by David Farrell Krell. New York: Harper & Row, 1977.

Hirschman, Albert O. *The Passions and the Interests: Political Arguments for Capitalism before Its Triumph.* Princeton: Princeton University Press, 1977.

Hoffman, Donna L. and Thomas P. Novak. "Marketing in Hypermedia Computer-Mediated Environments." Working

Paper No. 1, July 1995, Research Program on Marketing in Computer-Mediated Environments, Owen Graduate School of Management, Vanderbilt University.

Holbrook, Morris B. "Introduction: The Esthetic Imperative in Consumer Research." In *Symbolic Consumer Behavior* edited by Elizabeth C. Hirschman and Morris B. Holbrook. Ann Arbor: Association for Consumer Research, 1980.

Huberman, Bernardo A., Daniel M. Romero and Fang Wu. "Crowdsourcing, Attention and Productivity." Social Computing Lab, HP Laboratories, Palo Alto, CA, September 12, 2008.

Kamenetz, Anya. "The Perils and Promise of the Reputation Economy." *Fast Company* 131 (December 2008): www.fastcompany.com/magazine/131/on-the-internet-everyone-knows-youre-a-dog.html.

Kelly, Kevin. *Out of Control: The New Biology of Machines, Social Systems and the Economic World.* Reading: Addison-Wesley, 1994.

———. "Evidence of a Global SuperOrganism." The Technium (October 24, 2008): www.kk.org/thetechnium/archives/2008/10/evidence_of_a_g.php.

Kim, Peter with Chris Charron, et al. "Reinventing the Marketing Organization." Forrester Research July 13, 2006.

Krebs, Valdis. "Social Network Analysis, A Brief Introduction." Ornet.com. www.orgnet.com/sna.html.

Krueger, Myron W. "Responsive Environments." In *The New Media Reader* edited by Noah Wardrip-Fruin and Nick Montfort. Cambridge, MA: The MIT Press, 2003.

Kula, Witold. *Measures and Men.* Princeton: Princeton University Press, 1986.

Kumar, Krishan. *Prophecy and Progress: The Sociology of Industrial and Post-Industrial Society.* New York: Penguin, 1978.

Lampel J. and A. Bhalla. "The Role of Status Seeking in Online Communities: Giving the Gift of Experience." *Journal of Computer-Mediated Communication,* 12(2) (2007): article 5.

Leadbeater, Charles. *We-Think: Mass Innovation, Not Mass Production: The Power of Mass Creativity.* London, Profile Books, 2008.

Lears, T. J. Jackson. "From Salvation to Self-Realization: Advertising and the Therapeutic Roots of Consumer Culture, 1880–1930." In *The Culture of Consumption: Critical Essays in American History* edited by T. J. Jackson Lears and Richard Wrightman Fox. New York: Pantheon, 1983.

Leibniz, Gottfried Wilhelm. "The Method of Mathematics." In *Preface to the General Science* translated by Roger Bishop Jones.   www.rbjones.com/rbjpub/philos/classics/leibniz/meth_math.htm.

Leonard, Dorothy. "The Limitations of Listening." *Harvard Business Review* January 2002.

Levine, Rick, et al. *The Cluetrain Manifesto: The End of Business as Usual.* Cambridge, MA: Perseus Books, 1999.

Levy, Pierre. *Collective Intelligence: Mankind's Emerging World in Cyberspace.* New York: Plenum, 1997.

Li, Charlene with Josh Bernoff, Remy Fiorentino and Sarah Glass. "Social Technographics: Mapping Participation in Activities Forms the Foundation of a Social Strategy." *Forrester Research* April 19, 2007.

Longley, Paul A. and Graham Clarke, eds. *GIS for Business and Service Planning.* New York: John Wiley & Sons, 1995.

MacPherson, C. B. *The Political Theory of Possessive Individualism: Hobbes to Locke.* Oxford: Oxford University Press, 1962.

Madden, Mary et. al. *Digital Footprints: Online Identity Management and Search in the Age of Transparency.* Washington, DC: Pew Internet & American Life Project (2007): www.pewInternet.org/PPF/r/229/report_display.asp.

Manski, Charles F. "Interpreting the Predictions of Prediction Markets" (August 2005): www.aeaweb.org/annual_mtg_papers/2006/0106_1015_0703.pdf.

Marshall, Alfred. *Principles of Economics.* [1890] London: Macmillan, 1920.

Mauss, Marcel. *The Gift: The Form and Reason for Exchange in Archaic Societies.* New York: W. W. Norton, 2000. Originally, "Essai sur le don. Forme et raison de l'échange dans les sociétés archaïques," *L'Année Sociologique.* Nouvelle Serie, Tome 1. Paris: Librairie Félix Alcan, 1925.

Marchand, Roland. *Advertising the American Dream: Making Way for Modernity, 1920–1940.* Berkeley: University of California Press, 1985.

McLuhan, Marshall. *Understanding Media: The Extensions of Man.* New York: McGraw-Hill, 1964.

Mell, Patricia. "Seeking Shade in a Land of Perpetual Sunlight: Privacy as Property in the Electronic Wilderness." *Berkeley Technology Law Journal* vol. 11 (1996): www.law.berkeley.edu/journals/btlj/articles/vol11/Mell.pdf.

Miller, Peter. "Accounting and Objectivity: The Invention of Calculating Selves and Calculable Spaces." In *Rethinking Objectivity* edited by Allan Megill. Durham: Duke University Press, 1994.

Mosco, Vincent and Janet Wasko, eds. *The Political Economy of Information.* Madison: University of Wisconsin Press, 1988.

Naone, Erica, "Who Owns Your Friends? Social-networking sites are fighting over control of users' personal information." *Technology Review,* July/August 2008.

———. "Searching for Humans." *Technology Review* (August 20, 2007): www.technologyreview.com/communications/19270/.

"Online Brand Reviewers Anxious To Help Other Buyers." MediaPost (December 18, 2007): www.mediapost.com/blogs/research_brief/.

O'Reilly, Tim. "What is Web 2.0." O'Reilly: http://oreilly.com/web2/archive/what-is-web-20.html.

Page, Scott. *The Difference: How the Power of Diversity Creates Better Groups, Firms, Schools and Society.* Princeton University Press, 2007.

Patriquin, Alex. "Connecting the Social Graph: Member Overlap." Compete (November 12, 2007): http://blog. compete.com/2007/11/12/connecting-the-social-graph-member-overlap.

Pennock, David M., et al. "The Real Power of Artificial Markets." *Science* (February 2001): 987–988.

Pickles, John, ed. *Ground Truth: The Social Implications of Geographic Information Systems.* New York: Guilford Press, 1995.

Pircher, Wolfgang. "Tours Through the Back-Country of Imperfectly Informed Society." In *The Ideology of the Information Age* edited by Jennifer Daryl Slack and Fred Fejes. Norwood: Ablex Publishing Company, 1987.

Porter, Theodore M. "Objectivity as Standardization: The Rhetoric of Impersonality in Measurement, Statistics and Cost-Benefit Analysis." In *Rethinking Objectivity* edited by Allan Megill. Durham: Duke University Press, 1994.

Poster, Mark. *The Mode of Information: Post-Structuralism and Social Context.* Chicago: University of Chicago Press, 1990.

———. *What's the Matter with the Internet?* Minneapolis: University of Minnesota Press, 2001.

Prahalad, C. K. and Venkat Ramaswamy. *The Future of Competition: Co-creating Unique Value with Customers.* Cambridge: Harvard Business School Press, 2004.

ProjectVRM. http://cyber.law.harvard.edu/projectvrm.

Resnick, Paul, et al. "Reputation Systems: Facilitating Trust in Internet Interactions": www.si.umich.edu/~presnick/papers/cacm00/reputations.pdf.

Rheingold, Howard. *Virtual Community: Homesteading on the Electronic Frontier.* Cambridge, MA: The MIT Press, 2000.

Rhodes, Matt. "Insight from Online Communities: 4. Rating and Voting." Marketing and Strategy Innovation (January 28, 2009): www.futurelab.net/blogs/marketing-strategy-innovation/2009/01/insight_from_online_communitie.html.

Rothschild, Michael. *Bionomics: Economy as Ecosystem.* NY: Henry Holt, 1990.

Salvaggio, Jerry L. "Projecting a Positive Image of the Information Society." In *The Ideology of the Information Age* edited by Jennifer Daryl Slack and Fred Fejes. Norwood: Ablex Publishing Company, 1987.

Sanchez, Julian. "Mapping the Blogosphere with spinning brain of colored dots." Ars Technica (December 21, 2008): http://arstechnica.com/old/content/2008/12/mapping-the-blogosphere-with-spinning-brain-of-colored-dots.ars.

Schroeder, Stan."20 Ways To Aggregate Your Social Networking Profiles." Mashable (July 17, 2007): http://mashable.com/2007/07/17/social-network-aggregators/.

Schudson, Michael. *Advertising, the Uneasy Persuasion: Its Dubious Impact on American Society.* New York: Basic Books, 1984.

Schumpeter, Joseph. *Capitalism, Socialism and Democracy.* New York: Harper & Row, 1942.

Searls, Doc. "Building the Intention Economy." ProjectVRM Blog (September 14, 2008): http://blogs.law.harvard.edu/vrm/2008/09/14/building-the-intention-economy/.

Servan-Schreiber, Emile, et al. "Prediction Markets: Does Money Matter." *Electronic Markets* 14 (September 2004).

Shirky, Clay. *Here Comes Everybody: The Power of Organizing Without Organizations.* New York: Penguin, 2008.

———. "Ontology is Overrated: Categories, Links, and Tags." Clay Shirky's Writings About the Internet: http://shirky.com/writings/ontology_overrated.html.

Silver, Allan. "'Two Different Sorts of Commerce'—Friendship and Strangership in Civil Society." In *Public and Private in Thought and Practice: Perspectives on a Grand Dichotomy* edited by Jeff Weintraub and Krishan Kumar. Chicago: University of Chicago Press, 1997.

Simmel, Georg. "Individual and Society in Eighteenth- and Nineteenth-Century Views of Life." In *The Sociology of*

Georg Simmel, translated and edited by Kurt H. Wolff. New York: The Free Press, 1967.

Slater, Jan S. "Qualitative Research in Advertising." In *How Advertising Works: The Role of Research* edited by John Philip Jones. Thousand Oaks: Sage Publications, 1988.

Smith, Justin. "Facebook's 'Inside Sociologist' Shares Stats on Users' Social Behavior." Inside Facebook (February 27, 2009): www.insidefacebook.com/2009/02/27/facebooks-in-house-sociologist-shares-stats-on-users-social-behavior/.

Solzenitsyn, Alexander. *Cancer Ward.* New York: Farrar Straus and Giroux: 1999.

Starr, Paul and Ross Corson. "Who Will Have the Numbers? The Rise of the Statistical Services Industry and the Politics of Public Data." In *The Politics of Numbers* edited by William Alonso and Paul Starr. New York: Russell Sage Foundation, 1987.

Surowiecki, James. *The Wisdom of Crowds.* New York: Anchor, 2005.

Taylor, Charles. *Sources of the Self: The Making of Modern Identity.* Cambridge, MA: Harvard University Press, 1989.

Temkin, Bruce. *The 6 Laws of Customer Experience: The Fundamental Truths that Define How Organizations Treat Customers.* http://experiencematters.files.wordpress.com/2009/05/the-6-laws-of-customer-experience_v8b.pdf.

Thomke, Stefan and Eric Von Hippel. "Customers as Innovators: A New Way to Create Value." *Harvard Business Review* (April 2002).

Trow, George W. S., *Within the Context of No Context.* New York: Atlantic Monthly Press, 1997.

Turner, Michael A. and Robin Varghese. *Making Sense of the Privacy Debate: A Comparative Analysis of Leading Consumer Privacy Studies.* New York: The Direct Marketing Association, 2001.

Turkle, Sherry, *Life on the Screen: Identity in the Age of the Internet.* New York: Simon & Schuster, 1995.

Walker, Rob. "The Corporate Manufacture of Word of Mouth." *The New York Times Magazine* (December 5, 2004).

Warner, Fara. "Don't Shout, Listen." *Fast Company,* no. 49 (July 2001).

Washburn, Sherwood. "Tools and Human Evolution." *Scientific American* 203 (September 1960): 63–75.

Watkins, Jennifer. "Prediction Markets as an Aggregation Mechanism for Collective Intelligence." Proceedings of 2007 UCLA Lake Arrowhead Human Complex Systems Conference. http://repositories.cdlib.org/hcs/WorkingPapers2/JHW2007.

Watkins, J. W. N. "Philosophy and Politics in Hobbes." *Philosophical Quarterly* vol. v (1959): 125–146.

Watts, Duncan J. *Six Degrees: The Science of a Connected Age.* New York: W. W. Norton, 2003.

Webster, Frank. *Theories of the Information Society.* London: Routledge, 2002.

Weinberger, David. *Everything is Miscellaneous: The Power of the New Digital Disorder.* New York: Henry Holt & Co., 2007.

Weiss, Michael. *The Clustering of America.* New York: Harper & Row, 1988.

Whitehead, Alfred North. *Science and the Modern World.* New York: Macmillan, 1925.

Williams, Raymond. *Culture and Society, 1780–1950.* New York: Harper & Row, 1966.

Wolfers, J. and E. Zitzewitz. "Interpreting Prediction Market Prices as Probabilities." http://bpp.wharton.upenn.edu/jwolfers/Papers/InterpretingPredictionMarketPrices.

INDEX